NEW VIEWPOINTS ON
THE SPANISH COLONIZATION OF AMERICA

New Viewpoints on

THE SPANISH COLONIZATION OF AMERICA

By

Silvio Zavala

Philadelphia

UNIVERSITY OF PENNSYLVANIA PRESS

London: Humphrey Milford: Oxford University Press

1943

Manufactured in the United States of America

ACKNOWLEDGMENT

THE Carnegie Endowment for International Peace, through the Director of its Division of Economics and History, Dr. James T. Shotwell, provided the funds that made it possible to publish this volume. An English translation of the original Spanish text was prepared for the Endowment by Mrs. Joan Coyne. Professors Francis S. Philbrick and Arthur P. Whitaker, of the University of Pennsylvania, aided in revising the manuscript and in seeing it through the press. I wish to express my very warm thanks to the above-mentioned for the aid they have given me in the preparation and publication of this volume.

S. Z.

CONTENTS

INTRODUCTION

IN the years 1941 and 1942 I was invited to give several series of lectures on Spain's conquest and colonization of the New World. Some of these were delivered in the University of Guadalajara, under the auspices of the College of Mexico. Others constituted a part of a winter lecture course offered by the School of Law of the National University of Mexico, at the invitation of the Director of the Law School, Professor Vicente Peniche López. Finally, the Director of the Division of Economics and History of the Carnegie Endowment for International Peace, Dr. James T. Shotwell, invited me to give several lectures before student bodies in the United States. For this purpose I prepared lectures on various aspects of the Conquest, the enslavement of the Indians, the *encomiendas,* the labor of the natives, and the social experiments which accompanied or followed the Conquest.

These lectures have been brought together in the present volume. The reader will find that they are works of synthesis and interpretation rather than original contributions to knowledge and that they are not accompanied by the usual apparatus of scholarship. The reader who desires a more detailed discussion of these topics can find it in the various monographs that I have prepared, several of which have already been published, and the rest of which are scheduled for appearance in the near future.

The publication of my lectures in their present form seemed desirable because as a rule erudite works of a narrow scope are of interest to only a handful of specialists and seldom present the broad results of investigations. At times, it is more useful to bring together the results of these microscopic studies in order to show, as clearly as possible, the larger pattern of knowledge and ideas to which each study has contributed. Only in this way can the conclusions of an investigation be made to interest a more widely educated public outside the ranks of research workers.

It is not my purpose either to recite isolated facts or to deliver myself of facile generalizations, but to study some of the institutions that were characteristic of Spanish-Indian relationships in colonial America. I therefore examine the influential ideas of the period of conquest and colonization, the laws that governed the relationships between the newcomers bred in European culture and the aborigines of the New World, and the difficult problem of applying European law in the colonial environment.

It will be observed that I stress the social point of view as a means of focalizing the study of colonization as a process. In doing so, I point out certain errors that have resulted from applying predominantly political criteria, as our nineteenth-century historians have done with a few notable exceptions, in interpreting the colonial past of Spanish America.

Most of these historians have believed that the colonial period was a long age of lethargy and of scanty interest, sharply separated from the subsequent history of the Spanish-American peoples by their declarations of independence from Spain. The three colonial centuries were described as a mere prelude to the real historical drama initiated by the liberators in the early nineteenth century.

The fact is, however, that the great dates of political history do not always mark great changes in the social field. And while it is true that the colonial period offers a less animated picture than the national period, with its constitution-making, its *pronunciamientos,* and its frequent civil and international wars, we must not forget that the roots of present-day Spanish-American society lie deep in the colonial past and that this society developed a unique character which, to a great extent, still endures after more than a century of constant political agitation.

The reader of this study should keep in mind two important facts which help to explain both the character of Spanish-American society and the difference between it and society in the United States. In the first place, the European heritage of Spanish America was very different from that of the United States. This was not only because the former came from Spain rather than from England but also because it originated in the Europe of the fifteenth and sixteenth centuries, whereas that of the United States originated in the Europe of the seventeenth and eighteenth centuries. The colonization of America by Spain was already under way by 1500; that by England was not begun until after 1600. The intervening years were marked by a transformation of European life and culture. This transformation was an integral part of the original heritage of the English colonies, but it was accorded a different reception in the older Spanish colonies.

In the second place, social development in some of the most important Spanish colonies (notably Mexico and Peru) was shaped by a factor that did not exist in the English colonies, namely, the presence of highly developed, indigenous cultures which possessed in their own right a respectable past.

In some cases the cultural pattern of Spanish America was further complicated by the addition of African strains, and the fusion of these diverse elements produced a society very different from that of English America, which drew its inspiration mainly from the principles of the Reformation and of Rationalism.

This obvious diversity between English and Spanish America has been interpreted in various ways, according to the cultural background of the critics and their viewpoints in the field of human values. There are those who hold that Hispanic culture and its American derivatives constitute an "error," the gravity of which is in direct proportion to their departure from the chosen English model. Others think that this model, because of intrinsic and fundamental defects, is approaching a definitive crisis and that at such a moment the spiritual resources of the other culture, once condemned, regain inestimable value.

What the historian cannot overlook is that English America, although not free from impediments such as the extensive development within it of Negro slavery, developed a civilization more in conformity with the nineteenth-century idea of progress. In contrast with it, there emanated from the historical and cultural organization of the Spanish, Portuguese, and French colonies of America, societies less satisfactory from the point of view of the progressivist ideal but in other respects more mature and humane, as was to be expected of a deeper-rooted and more complex organic past. If it be necessary to cite examples in order to clarify this judgment, it may suffice to mention the flexibility shown by the Brazilian and Mexican cultures in harmonizing their diverse racial components; the inclination in Spanish-American countries to self-criticism which proscribes dogmatic and superficial optimism; their reserves of patience revealed in surmounting historical reverses; their disinterested appreciation of beauty, and so on.

In conclusion, we are justified in saying that these two American cultures possess heritages of potentialities and limitations of markedly different character. A study of their history cannot only contribute to a clearer understanding of each but can also make it easier for them to live in harmony with each other.

· I ·

THE LEGAL CLAIMS OF SPAIN IN THE INDIES

THE legal problems of sixteenth-century Spain are closely connected with theological ideas. They are also linked with political and moral philosophy. Hence, no sooner do we pose the first questions regarding the right of conquest than we find that the main conclusions do not always proceed from the jurists. It was mainly the task of the latter to solve the legal difficulties peculiar to conquest and colonization, but important contributions were also made by men outstanding in other fields, such as the theologian Vitoria and the political philosopher Sepúlveda.

I sound this warning in order that no one may for a moment imagine that we depart from the history of Spanish America, which we have proposed to explore, when we pause before these ideological questions of European culture. On the contrary, if we omitted them we should lack almost all the elements necessary to an understanding of the problem.

We must also remember that it is the military phase of the Conquest which has been most generally studied, and that in the field of literature it is the epic which has been stressed. But an account of the Conquest limited to acts of violence between the European and the native races is a most incomplete one. For example, it does not embrace the juridical doubts aroused by the fact of Spain's setting out to conquer America. Neither does it take into consideration the laws constantly promulgated by the Crown with the purpose of regulating the relationships brought about by the Conquest. Furthermore, even within the field of action not all deeds were military. As a swift glance through any historical work referring to the period of the Conquest will show, economic and social phenomena occurred in conjunction with strictly military action.

Hence, the concept we wish to establish at the outset is not that of a strictly military conquest. Our mode of approach to this historical problem is to inquire into the background of the ideas bearing upon it, the evolution of thought that accompanied it, and the various modifications and shadings which can be distinguished in an episode so complex and of such vast consequences to American and world history.

How can the theme of the relationship between the Spaniards and the natives be stated in terms of the legal ideas of the time? Any conquest, even in our time, soon becomes enveloped in a complex of ideas projected to explain it. Today this task is performed by newspapers and many other instruments of publicity; in the sixteenth century it was performed mainly by the writers of treatises. Consequently, we must seek to determine the lines of thought most characteristic of these treatises.

Everything pondered and written in the sixteenth century clearly reveals as a dominant note concern with the relationship between a Christian world (or, if you prefer, a European world) and a world described as infidel or heathen. The problem of intercourse between Christian and infidel had arisen in Europe long before the discovery of America. At least as early as the thirteenth century there was a very considerable aggregate of doctrine, built up by prominent churchmen and secular jurists, dealing with the manner in which this problem should be solved. For example, Henry of Susa Cardinal Bishop of Ostia, who is best known among students of canonical law as Ostiensis, voiced a theory which was to be utilized three centuries later when America was discovered. He maintained that, in accordance with natural law and *jus gentium,* heathen peoples had their own political jurisdiction and their own possessions before Christ came into the world. But when this occurred, all the powers and the rights of dominion held by heathen peoples passed to Christ, who, according to this doctrine, became lord over the earth, both in the spiritual and the temporal sense. Christ delegated that supreme dominion to his successors – first St. Peter and later the Popes – so that at any given moment they had the legal right and power to annul the existing jurisdictions of the infidel. And the non-Christians would have no right to retain the jurisdictions which had been conceded to them under the *jus gentium* prior to the division of the world into Christian and heathen zones.

The importance of this opinion is great, for when the Catholic monarchs found themselves preoccupied with the juridical problems of America, they consulted various authorities regarding the soundest basis on which to rest the rights which Spain, by her acts in America, was constantly acquiring. Several of the most important theologians of the court and one outstanding jurist, Juan López de Palacios Rubios, referred to the thesis stated in the thirteenth century and were of the opinion that the case of America could be accounted for only by an exercise of that right which belonged to Christendom. That is, when Pope Alexander VI issued his pontifical bulls in favor of the Spanish monarchs, he was putting into execution the doctrine of the subordination of the rights of the heathen world to the authorities of Christendom.

Palacios Rubios wrote a treatise, still unpublished, which was entitled "Of the Ocean Isles." The Spanish jurist fully expounded the doctrine already formulated in the thirteenth century to solve the relationship between the Christian and the infidel worlds within the juridical field. But he did not stop with the writing of the treatise. With the consent of the monarchs he later wrote a document, the *requerimiento,* which all the conquistadors were to use as a charter establishing the rights of Spain in America. In this requerimiento he again expounded the doctrine of the division of the world into Christian and heathen, and stated the right of Christ, through his representative the Pope, to hold the infidel world in subjugation.

The following quotations from this famous document (as translated into English by Sir Arthur Helps) will show how much weight the application of such ideas came to have in the field of law. After explaining the creation of the world according to the Bible, the requerimiento declares that Christ raised St. Peter above all other men:

And moreover, he commanded him to fix his seat at Rome as the fittest place for governing the world, but he also permitted him to establish a seat in any other part of the world and to judge and govern all men – Christians, Moors, Jews, Gentiles, and whatever other sect or creed there may be.

The document went on to state how a certain Pope, as ruler of the world, had given all the isles and mainlands of the Ocean Sea to the Catholic sovereigns of Spain. The Spanish commander was required to read this document to the Indians and then to give them time to understand and deliberate upon what had been said to them, calling upon them to acknowledge the Church as sovereign mistress of the world and the Pope in her name, and the King in his place as their lord.

If you do so [the Indians were to be told], His Majesty will greet you with all love and affection and leave your wives and children free so that you may do with them as you wish, and will give you many privileges and exemptions. He will not compel you to turn Christian unless you, informed of the truth, wish to be converted to our Holy Catholic Faith, as have so many inhabitants of other isles, but if you do, His Majesty will show you many favors. But if you do not, or if you maliciously delay in doing so, by the help of God, I will enter into your lands and will subdue you to the yoke of obedience to the Church and to their Majesties and I will take your wives and children and make slaves of them, and will sell them as such, and will take all your goods and do you all the mischief I can, as to vassals who will not obey and will not receive their lord. And I protest that all the death and destruction which may come from this is your own fault, and not His Majesty's or mine or that of my men.

Most of the Spanish conquistadors made use of this document. For example, when the Governor of Cuba, Diego Velásquez, sent Hernán Cortés to conquer Mexico, he gave him certain instructions directing him to tell the Indians that he was sent in the name of the King of Spain to

> require them to bow beneath his yoke and service and royal protection and that they may be sure that if they do this, and if they serve him well and faithfully, they will be well rewarded and favored and sheltered against their enemies by His Highness and by me, acting in his name.

First, however, Cortés was to tell them that the King of Spain was very powerful, "whose vassals and subjects we and they are." In this way, even before contact was established between the Spaniards and the Indians, the latter were regarded as subject to Spanish jurisdiction.

In accordance with these precedents, Cortés was able to write in his "Letters of Accounting" to Charles V that he ordered certain Indians:

> That within three days they should appear before me to yield obedience to Your Highness and to offer themselves as vassals, with the warning that if the time I allowed them were to pass and they were to fail to come I would go upon them and would proceed against them as against persons in rebellion who refused to submit themselves to the dominion of Your Highness. And to that end I sent them an order signed with my name and with that of an official scrivener with a long relation regarding Your Majesty and telling them about my coming, and that all these regions and many larger lands and fiefs belonged to Your Majesty and that those who wished to become vassals would be honored and favored but that on the contrary, those who remained rebels would be punished according to justice.

What possible meaning could the word "rebel" have to a chieftain who had never heard of the Spaniards before this first contact with Cortés? If there was no previous right of the Church delegated to the Spanish monarchs, which right

Cortés had come to execute, it would be impossible to claim that the Indians committed an act of rebellion in refusing to accept Christian sovereignty. You will note that the account which Hernán Cortés sent his King was an official one explaining to him how he had conducted his conquest. If he had not considered that the ideas expressed were the correct ideas of his time, he would have taken good care not to express them so frankly to one who had the power to judge his acts.

Let us now consider the effects of the proclamation from the point of view of the heathen. We shall see that its application was neither easy nor peaceful.

The historians of the Indies have preserved some very valuable evidence of the application of its principles. When Pedrarias Dávila set out to conquer Castilla del Oro, or Darien, he carried the proclamation with him and ordered one of his captains to read it to the Indians of a certain province. They replied that what the captain had told them of the existence of only one God who ruled Heaven and earth seemed very good to them, for that was how it should be; but that the Pope had given away what was not his, and that the King must be a crazy man to ask for and to accept such a thing since he demanded what belonged to others. Let the captain try to take it and they would put his head on a pole as they had done before with the heads of other enemies, which they showed him.

Gonzalo Fernández de Oviedo, a historian and soldier, tells us also regarding the expedition of Pedrarias:

> The governor ordered me to bring with me the written proclamation treating of the Indians and he gave it to me with his own hands as though I understood the Indians well enough to read it to them, or as though we might find someone there to make them understand, provided they wanted to hear it. For showing them the paper on which it was written had little to do with the case. In the presence of all I said to him: "Sir, it seems to me that these Indians do not care to hear the theology of this proclamation, nor do you have anyone who will make them understand it. You

should order it kept until we have caught some of these Indians, put them in a cage, and slowly taught them, and the bishop shall have made it clear to them." And I gave him the proclamation and he took it amid much laughter from him and all the others who heard me. Later, in 1516, I asked Dr. Palacios Rubios (for he had written that proclamation) if the consciences of Christians were satisfied with that proclamation and he said yes, if the terms of the proclamation were followed. But it seemed to me that he laughed often as I was telling him of that military expedition and of others which certain captains had later made: I could laugh much harder at him and his learning (for he was reputed to be a great man and as such held a place in the royal Council of Castile) if he really believed that the Indians were going to understand what that proclamation says until after the passage of many years.

Bernal Díaz, in his history, states that on one occasion there was no interpreter to make known to the Indians what the Spaniards wanted, and the captain sent them a paper by messenger. It was known that they could not read it, but the historian of New Spain reasoned that, as they could see that it was a paper from Castile, they would understand that it was a command and thus it would have the desired effect.

If criticisms had amounted only to this — namely, to the difficulty of putting a legal principle into practice — Dr. Palacios Rubios might justly have reasoned as he replied to Oviedo: "The principles are good, but the application is difficult; if the captains follow the order, I have solved the problem in accordance with the law."[1] But such a manner of establishing the justice of the Conquest was not satisfactory to critical European opinion.

Beginning with the thirteenth century itself, in which the position taken by Palacios Rubios found its origin, we encounter doctrinal inquiries of another kind which leave us in greater perplexity regarding the problem of the relation between Christians and heathen. From this point of view one of

[1] This is a paraphrase, not a direct quotation.

the most important writers of treatises is Thomas Aquinas, not only because of the very decided ideas regarding the heathen found in his *Summa* but also because, as is well known, the Thomist doctrine became one of the bases of instruction in the universities of Europe. Hence the theologians and jurists who were later to study the American problem generally had recourse to Scholasticism, and referred to the *Summa* of Aquinas.

What, then, do we find in the *Summa* with respect to this delicate problem of the conduct of the Christian world, juridically considered, toward the heathen? One question involving theft and plunder is whether in all cases such acts are sins, or whether in some cases they may not be so. The question whether it is just to take from another what is not his is applied to infidels in a charter in which Aquinas, following St. Augustine, assumes the infidels' possession to be wrongful. St. Thomas reasons that whenever infidels possess a thing wrongfully it may be taken from them, but it is not right to do so in cases of lawful possession since that would involve violence. In keeping with this basic distinction, when the Christian faces the pagan world the former must ask itself by what right pagans enjoy their political hierarchies and their dominion. According to Thomist doctrine, the answer to the question whether or not Christians should proceed against them depends upon the solution of this problem.

In other parts of the *Summa* St. Thomas turns back to this important problem of paganism and asks himself whether the state of being heathen is not itself a sin for which the Christian world may punish them. He makes another distinction and raises the question whether or not their lack of faith is of the completely negative type. If the heathen have never heard of the Christian faith, there is no sin, nor any reason for punishment. But if the lack of faith is of the aggressive type and the infidel are like the Saracens who overran Europe, constantly attacking the Christians, then there is sufficient cause for punishment.

As to the doubt whether infidels can be compelled to accept the Christian faith, he declares that they cannot be forced to believe, for belief is a voluntary act.

He elucidates likewise the question whether the infidel may be allowed preferment or sovereignty over the faithful, as in a kingdom whose subjects are Christian and the rulers infidel. Here Aquinas makes an important statement: Dominion and sovereignty over others is an invention of human law, but the distinction between faithful and infidel is a law of divine origin. The latter, which proceeds from God, does not destroy human law which proceeds from human reason. Hence the relationship between faithful and infidel, considered by itself, does not preclude the sovereignty and preferment of infidel over faithful. St. Thomas tempers this doctrine with one serious reservation, however. He says that the right of the infidel to sovereignty over Christians can be removed through an ordinance of the Church in exercise of its divine authority, for infidels, by reason of their lack of faith, deserve to lose power over the faithful. Consequently Thomist doctrine contains some principles susceptible of a later liberal development, but it also admits that there are limitations upon the rights of pagans.

We have paused to consider the *Summa* because, as we shall see, European theologians and jurists who considered the problem of the American heathen in the sixteenth century referred constantly to its principles and so interpreted it as to sustain their own conclusions.

When, as already explained, the doctrine of Palacios Rubios began to awaken uneasiness in men's minds and not merely to perplex administrators, Cardinal Cajetan, one of the great commentators upon the *Summa* of St. Thomas, held that a distinction must be made between various types of infidel. There were those who were in fact and by right the subjects of Christian princes — for example, the Jews, heretics, and Moors who lived in Christian lands. There were other infidels who were by right, but not in fact, the subjects of Christian princes — for example, those who occupied Christian lands. In the course of his argument the wars against

Mohammedans were mentioned. But there was a third group of infidels who were not subjects of Christian princes, either by right or in fact – for example, the pagans who never were subjects of the Roman Empire, and the inhabitants of lands which had never heard the name of Christ. The latter did not lack the right to govern because of their lack of faith, for such right proceeds from positive law and faith is a matter of divine law, which does not destroy the positive law. Against such heathen no king or emperor or even the Roman Church might declare war with the purpose of occupying their territories or of holding them in temporal subjection, for there was no just cause for such war. Christ, to whom were granted all powers over Heaven and earth, did not send armed soldiers to take possession of the world. Rather he sent saintly preachers, like sheep among wolves. The employment of any other means of spreading the Christian faith would constitute a grievous sin. Christians would not become lawful lords over such pagans but would, on the contrary, commit a great theft and would be morally bound to make reparation. To the heathen should be sent good men to convert them to God through precept and example, and not people who would oppress, exploit, scandalize, and subjugate them in the manner of the Pharisees.

One of the teachers in the University of Paris, John Major, also took this serious problem under consideration and commented upon some of the principles enunciated in the *Summa Theologica*. He believed that the kingdom of Christ is not of this world and that the Pope was named only a spiritual vicar. Contrary to the belief of Ostiensis, he did not recognize the Pope's temporal dominion over heathen peoples and also denied that the emperor was lord of all the earth. Regarding the American Indians, he reasoned that sovereignty, as St. Thomas said, was founded not upon faith nor upon charity which proceed from divine law, but upon titles of natural law under which the pagan might be entitled to liberty, property, and temporal power. He also admitted the distinction regarding the various types of infidel, explaining that there are infidels who possess Christian territories, such as the King of Memphis, who is popularly known as the Sultan of Syria, who rules over the Holy Land, Egypt, and Arabia. Likewise the Ottoman Turk controls Turkey and Greece, which were formerly owned by Christian princes. There are others who have obtained their territories not by conquest but through just heathen title to them. These may comport themselves in various ways: either they may permit the preaching of the Christian faith among them without despising Christ and his law, or they may oppose the establishment of the faith.

Examining the group of authors who are outstanding in Spanish-American history, we find the name of Las Casas. He believed that among the pagans who had never heard of Christ nor received the faith there were rightful lords, kings, and princes; and that their sovereignty, dignity, and royal eminence were derived from natural law and *jus gentium*. Obviously alluding to the doctrine of Ostiensis in order to combat it through its exponent, Palacios Rubios, Las Casas says that with the coming of Christ the heathen were not deprived of their sovereignty, either universally or privately. Any contrary opinion was impious.

If we go forward until we reach Francisco de Vitoria, it will be easy to see in his "Lectures on the Indians" that the entire first chapter is based upon those Thomist ideas according to which political organizations and rights to possession proceed from natural reason and human rights and are not divine in origin, and are compatible with the distinction between the infidel and the faithful. In Vitoria's lengthy analysis of all the claims which until then had been considered valid in justifying the Conquest, and in his rejection of them in the fundamental portion of his work entitled "Of Illegitimate Claims," we note that the universal temporal sovereignty of the Pope and of the emperor and all the other reasonings based upon the Indians' lack of faith are rejected.

In summary, what is the result of this very rapid examination of the two great attitudes adopted in the sixteenth century, on the basis of even older principles, with regard to the problem raised by the intrusion of Europeans into the heathen world of America?

In the first period we find an excessive universal affirmation of the temporal right of the Church, and hence of the kings who obtained their sovereignty through the Church. We also find a facile denial of the rights of the heathen people with whom contact was made. When, however, the practical difficulty of applying the requerimiento together with the best theoretical analysis of the problem began to destroy the foundations upon which the first school of thought rested, we find that Europeans themselves limited the scope of the temporal jurisdiction of Christendom and at the same time maintained that the rights of the heathen could and should be sustained. And when, on the one hand, they had limited their rights to expansion and, on the other hand, had buttressed the political and legal claims of the pagans, the problem was still further complicated. Henceforth the just claims which would be allowed according to these principles would be fewer, but they would be of world-wide application and of greater merit.

· II ·

THE PAPAL BULLS OF ALEXANDER VI RELATIVE TO THE INDIES

THE bulls of Pope Alexander VI dealing with the West Indies have been the subject of historical caricature rather than of serious investigation, as can be proved from books which still enjoy prestige today. These state that Alexander was of Spanish origin and hence inclined to favor the cause of Spain, and that he was on good terms with the Catholic monarchs. They also represent him as having made a gift of the West Indies to these friends of his, dividing the world by whim between them and the Portuguese. With one stroke he disposed of all political rights and sovereignty over the Indians, to the great indignation of all those who favored defending the rights of the natives and also of those foreign nations which, beginning with the sixteenth century, competed with Spain in world politics. Another popular interpretation is that since Spain and Portugal were rivals in the field of exploration and discovery, the Pope issued his bulls as an arbitrator of that conflict.

How much truth is there in these interpretations regarding the right of sovereignty and the arbitral award?

The first question we must answer is what historical rôle had the Papacy played in the matter of early discoveries and assignments of new lands previous to the discovery of America? For the bulls of Alexander are neither the first nor the only ones of this kind in existence. Since the sixteenth century it has been known that such antecedents existed, but a more complete list of them can now be drawn up with the aid of modern treatises, in particular those of the Belgian professor, Ernest Nys, who was one of the first to take a critical historical attitude toward the international problem of legal history involved in the bulls of Alexander VI.

In 1016 and 1049 the people of Pisa based claims upon apocryphal bulls regarding the Island of Sardinia. In 1155 Adrian IV granted Ireland to Henry II of England and his successors, on condition that they convert its inhabitants to the Catholic faith and that they pay a certain tribute to the Church as feudal dues. In 1344 Clement VI gave the principality of the Canary Islands to Luis de la Cerda, Count of Clermont and son of Alfonso of Castile, who had been expelled by Sancho IV. The Count was obliged to render homage to the Church in exchange. In the second decade of the fifteenth century, Martin V is supposed to have invested the King of Portugal with the right to all the lands discovered from Cape Bogador to India and to have adjured all kings, lords, and communities not to disturb the King in possession of these lands. In 1437 Pope Eugenius IV decided, on the advice of the Consistory of the Vatican regarding the expedition of Alfonso V of Portugal against the infidels of Tangiers, that if the infidels occupied Christian territories and had transformed the churches into mosques or had done wrong to the Christians or had shown themselves to be idolaters or had sinned against nature, just war could be waged against them, though it must be waged with piety and discretion. In 1452 Nicholas V, by virtue of his apostolic authority, permitted Alfonso of Portugal and his successors to attack and reduce to servitude the Saracens and other infidel enemies of Christ and to seize their lands and movable property. Similar bulls were issued by Calixtus III in 1456, by Pius II in 1459, and by Sixtus IV in 1481. The bulls relating to the West Indies were of the year 1493. In 1497 Pope Alexander VI issued another bull to King Manuel of Portugal in which he spoke of respecting the will of the infidels.

In view of this established attitude of the Papacy with regard to discoveries in Europe, Africa, and Asia, Professor Nys concludes that the act of the Pontiff respecting the lands discovered in America merits neither the excessive praise nor denunciation which have been heaped upon it. The attacks are without foundation, and so are the praises. The Pope, or rather the Papal Chancery, answered a petition for a grant with a patent modeled upon those which had frequently been issued on former occasions.

We must bear in mind also the notions of geography probably held by the Papal Chancery when the bulls regarding the Indies were issued. Columbus had just returned from his first voyage, and it was not yet known whether his discovery was of a great new world or of some islands near Asia. All that the Vatican documents show is that, as a consequence of information brought to Spain by the discoverer himself, there were remote and unknown mainlands and islands in a region never before explored or known, and that Columbus' men would seek other remote and unknown islands and mainlands which might lie toward India or toward some other region. We all know today the geographical importance of the discovery which Spain had sponsored and that, compared with it, the previous examples of Papal intervention were less significant. But this should not prevent us from agreeing that at the time when they were drawn up and issued, the geographical content of the bulls of Alexander VI relating to the West Indies was not substantially different from that of the earlier bulls mentioned above.

Before entering upon other historical and juridical considerations regarding the bulls of Alexander VI, we shall briefly review their contents. In the first place, we speak of the bulls in the plural although they are sometimes mentioned as a single pronouncement. We must, however, consider four proclamations. The first and second bear the date of May 3, 1493; the third appears to have been issued the next day. The three documents are similar in many respects, but there are appreciable differences. The fourth bull is dated September 26, 1493.[1]

The first bull mentions the discovery by Columbus and assigns the sovereignty of the new lands to the monarchs of Spain, Ferdinand and Isabella, citing previous grants in Africa in favor of the Crown of Portugal. The second and third bulls both represent a more elaborate rewriting of the first bull. They begin by referring to the great services rendered the Catholic Church by the Spanish monarchs through the conquest of the kingdom of Granada and the voyage of Columbus that led to the discovery of lands with inhabitants who might be persuaded to receive the faith. The monarchs of Spain desired to undertake the task of converting these people to Christianity, wherefore they presented their proposal to the Pope, who encouraged them in the enterprise and granted them broad powers as lords of the aforesaid territories in order to enable them to carry out their intent with greater freedom. The second document went on to mention the privileges granted to the monarchs of Portugal in Africa and to extend similar prerogatives to the Spanish monarchs in the lands discovered by Columbus. This paragraph does not appear in the third bull, but, on the other hand, this bull speaks of the "Line of Demarcation" which was to run from the North to the South Pole, at a distance of one hundred leagues west and south of any of the islands commonly known as the Azores and Cape Verdes. All the islands and mainlands discovered and to be discovered beyond that line in the aforesaid directions were to belong to Spain, provided that they were not in the actual possession of any Christian king or prince up to the date of Christmas of the year prior to the date of the bull. The Pope charged the monarchs to send wise and God-fearing men to implant Christianity among the inhabitants of the discovered places, and under pain of excommunication he forbade all persons, even though they might be of royal or imperial rank, to make use of such lands

[1] It is a well-known fact that the dates given these bulls are not the dates on which they were actually issued.

for markets or for any other purpose without special license from the monarchs of Spain. The fourth bull (September 26, 1493) amplified the previous grants to the Spanish monarchs. It authorized them to take possession of all islands and mainlands already discovered or to be discovered toward the west or south, whether in the western parts or in the regions south and east and in India, notwithstanding previous apostolic constitutions and ordinances or any grants and assignments of the aforesaid regions, provided, however, these grants should not have gone into effect through actual and effective possession.

Now, we may ask, what was the intention of the Pope in making the grants contained in the documents of 1493 to the monarchs of Spain, and with what authority were they issued? In the second and third bulls specific mention is made of "the authority of the omnipotent God delegated to us through Saint Peter, and of the Vicariate of Jesus Christ which we exercise on earth." It may be thought that the Roman Curia in speaking of this vicariate accepted the doctrine of the temporal universal sovereignty of the Papacy over the heathen world, of which Canon Ostiensis spoke in the thirteenth century and which the jurist, Palacios Rubios, accepted three centuries later. But it might also be, as other authors maintain, that the Pope intended to entrust the Spanish monarchs with only a missionary enterprise for the spread of the faith and that accordingly, acting entirely within his powers as the spiritual vicar of Christ, he granted a series of privileges of a temporal or quasi-temporal nature with regard to a spiritual matter and recommended especially that persons be sent out charged with the propagation of the faith. Las Casas argued that Alexander VI constituted the Spanish monarchs the founding apostles of the Indies.

The division of opinion among sixteenth-century writers of treatises regarding the true character and object of the Alexandrine bulls still exists among modern investigators, for while some fix their attention on the paragraphs in the bulls wherein the Pope says that he constitutes the Spanish monarchs and their successors the lords of the islands and mainlands discovered, "with full, free, ample, and absolute authority and jurisdiction," others concentrate their attention upon the religious clauses preceding the papal grants and on the obligation laid by these upon the Spanish sovereigns to send out apostles of the faith. Pedro Leturia, a distinguished modern writer, defends the latter opinion and states that the Papacy did not assert any direct power to annul or to declare null and void the sovereignty of the pagans or to transfer it to the faithful. The Pope did, however, confirm, by means of a missionary and international investiture, the acquisition of sovereignty over them which was assumed to have been already obtained by virtue of a gigantic crusade.

However, this brings us back to the problem of the relationships between Christians and infidels, which evidently is intimately linked to the bulls, especially the bull of Nicholas V, of 1452, already cited.

It is important to note that we are more concerned with the doctrine of the Roman Curia than with the personal ideas which may have been held by a pope like Alexander VI. As many historians have pointed out, it is very probable that he had no personal knowledge of the Spanish negotiation at any time in its course and that it was handled entirely by the officials of the Curia in accordance with the ordinary procedure. Even if this was not the case, the problem of Christian conduct toward heathen peoples had a history extending over several centuries, in the course of which it developed an institutional character which was not likely to be greatly modified by the personal character of an individual pope.

It is possible, on the other hand, that the ideas of the Roman Curia concerning its own power may have undergone an evolution in the course of centuries; nor can we ignore the fact that official Roman doctrine was necessarily made to cover cases differing from one another, whether because they referred to the thorny conflict between the spiritual and the temporal powers within Christendom or to varying types of heathen peoples.

E. Staedler states that the theory of the time of Gregory VII relative to the world primacy of the Church and the granting of fiefs to emperors and kings was supported in practice only when there was no opposition from the European temporal powers. When such opposition was shown, the domination of the Church boiled down to a position favoring the temporal jurisdiction of the Church as a form of political relationship with non-Christian countries over which the sovereignty of the Church and the propagation of the faith could be established.

The same author rigorously scrutinizes the wording used in the Alexandrine bulls, and he points out that the terms used in them are: *Donationis, concessionis, assignationis,* and not *donationis* alone. The separation of this one word from a sequence which is in fact indivisible has led to the interpretation of the bull in accordance with the common concept of a gift or a donation as in the Code of Justinian. But in fact its legal pedigree can be traced back to the long series of feudal investitures of laymen with estates of the Church.

The oldest antecedents of the formula used in such cases by the Papal Curia are found in usufructuary leases of land to Roman veterans under praetorian law. Later, German feudalism affected ceremonies of investiture and the formulas in charters of feoffment.

Grotius and other authors failed to perceive the true nature of the edict of Alexander VI, for they regarded it in the same light as donations made under the Roman civil law instead of relating it to the Roman praetorian law governing usufructuary grants and to feudal investiture.

In opposition to the viewpoint of Staedler, there is an observation made by Vander Linden to the effect that the term "investiture" figures in the first wording of the bull *Inter caetera* of May 3 but does not appear in the later Alexandrine texts relating to the rights of Spain. From this fact Vander Linden argues that the change was made in order "not to give grounds for supposing that a feudal investiture was contemplated."

But Staedler, who does not seem to have had Vander Linden's study in mind, develops his argument on the basis that the formula "to give, grant, and assign" is sufficiently characteristic of the feudal investiture. If Staedler's view is correct, it follows that the observation made by Vander Linden cannot be conceded the significance he attaches to it, since in spite of the textual difference noted by him it is still possible to regard the Alexandrine documents as belonging to the series of feudal patents.

This interpretation of the bulls leads us to another question: What exactly did the papal documents grant to the Catholic monarchs, or (following Staedler more precisely) with what did they invest the monarchs?

Under an interpretation favorable to the temporal domination of the Papacy over the world outside Christendom, the papal documents in question would be regarded as conferring full political rights, accompanied by all the territorial sovereignty exercised by any European monarch of the day. But in the eyes of treatise writers who champion the missionary interpretation, what was conferred was merely a sovereignty conditioned upon the serving of a religious aim and having validity only in so far as it was oriented toward that end.

We have now made it clear that the writers of the sixteenth century were not in agreement in regard to the conclusions that they drew from the bulls; but it is more important to ascertain what was the official interpretation placed by the Spanish Crown upon the type of investiture it had received from the Pope. There is no room for doubt on this point, for from the very beginning the Spanish monarchs considered themselves the political lords of the Indies, on the same footing as in their European realms. Moreover, there were treatise writers enjoying favor at the Court who hinted to the monarchs that even without the bulls they were complete lords of the new lands by virtue of their rights of discovery and occupation. Accordingly, the Spanish monarchs state in

Law I, Title I, Book III, of the *Recopilación de Indias* (Code of the Indies):

> Through donation of the Holy Apostolic See and other just and legitimate titles, we are lord of the West Indies, the Islands and mainlands of the Ocean Sea already discovered or to be discovered, and they are incorporated in our royal Crown of Castile.

But that the Spanish monarchs should have accepted the Alexandrine bulls, together with other patents referred to but not specified in the above-mentioned code, as assurance of their political sovereignty, does not mean that they would have denied the validity of the interpretation which emphasized the religious aspect of the grant. Other laws in the same code clearly accept the Catholic objectives of Spanish enterprise in the Indies, as well as the duty of the Crown, as charged by the Pope, to lend aid to the task of propagating the faith in the New World. Hence Professor de los Ríos speaks of a church state, that is, of a political organization which is invested with the transcendent purpose of the Church and which seeks to combine its secular functions with a religious mission. Hence the dual character, missionary and political, of the Spanish state in the Indies.

Passing from the examination of the bulls as titles to sovereignty, let us consider whether they actually constitute an arbitral decision. In spite of the fact that authorities from the earliest times have considered them to be such, historical evidence proves the contrary.

Leturia has noted that when the Pope intervened in the problems presented by the discoveries, he did not act as an arbitrator chosen by previous agreement between the parties in order to render a final decision. Rather, he acted as a previously constituted superior, missionary, and pacifying authority wielding the still formidable power of excommunication, whose favorable decision was sought in order to anticipate a rival power. Spain and Portugal regarded the pontifical prerogatives as merely a safeguard and definite sanction of their respective colonial rights.

The correspondence of the Catholic monarchs with Columbus, in which the bulls are mentioned, further weakens the case for regarding the Pope as an arbitrator in this affair. For even after the Pope sent the bulls to Spain, the tension between the Spanish and Portuguese monarchs continued and threatened a break which was avoided only by means of direct negotiations between the two powers. Just as there was no previous agreement to arbitrate before the Alexandrine bulls were issued, so their issuance failed to bring about the termination of the dispute.

Moreover, the Catholic monarchs frequently consulted Columbus regarding the geographical data necessary to obtain papal documents adequate to protect the rights of Spain. It is noted that the Line of Demarcation fixed by the bull of May 4, 1493, was suggested to the monarchs by the discoverer, and they sent it to Rome. But if one of the parties to the dispute was thus able to influence the drafting of the documents, it is easy to understand that they would have had no value as an arbitral award in the eyes of the other party. The influence of Columbus through the Catholic monarchs is seen again in the documents drawn by the Roman Curia when it amplified the rights of Spain in the bull of September 26, 1493. The monarchs knew that there might be important lands lying outside the dominion of Spain as established in the bull drawing the Line of Demarcation; they asked the opinion of the discoverer of America; and the modifications safeguarding the Spanish rights in a broader area were promptly granted in Rome.

Direct negotiations between the Spanish and Portuguese governments continued, and at last they signed the Treaty of Tordesillas, June 7, 1494. By its provisions the line was shifted to 370 leagues west of the Cape Verde Islands. This agreement was reached through direct negotiation between the two crowns without any intervention by the Pope. But in the last part of the document the contracting parties requested the Pope to confirm and approve the agreement by sending bulls to each of the parties and by threatening to punish anyone attempting to set it aside.

Likewise, when Charles V sold Molucca to the King of Portugal, April 22, 1529, the conditions of the sale were arrived at by agreement of both parties, and they then agreed that the treaty should be regarded as a pontifical decision and confirmed by an apostolic bull as a means of further corroborating and strengthening it. Possibly these concluding clauses gave rise to an association of ideas which passed on to posterity and which linked together agreements between the Iberian rulers and the notion of a Roman court of arbitration.

The truth of the matter is that even in the sixteenth century this interpretation began to gain strength among European writers, and it soon developed into a belief that a partition of the world had taken place and that the Pope had made the rulers of Spain and Portugal a stupendous gift.

Incorrect views regarding the right of sovereignty and papal arbitration are not the outgrowth of historical errors alone but of powerful political and religious considerations also. At the time of the Alexandrine bulls, Europe was passing from the feudal age into the period of great, modern, monarchical states. The politics of the balance of power began to prevail, and the excessive strength of Spain proved incompatible with it. The farsightedness of the Iberian countries in the realm of discovery began to yield them considerable advantages in the fields of politics, navigation, and commerce. Other powerful states such as Holland, France, and England began a long struggle to destroy the Iberian ascendancy, which was prejudicial to them. Thus Francis I of France said relative to the Alexandrine bulls: "The sun shines on me as well as on others. I should be very happy to see the clause in Adam's will which excluded me from my share when the world should come to be divided."

The authors then writing about the bulls were not free from political passions aroused by a theme of such transcendent importance. Many of these authors attacked their validity and made them objects of satire; while Spanish writers of treatises, including Solórzano, who had maintained that the monarchs had a right to the Indies even without the bulls, defended their validity. They took the position that the Pope had the proper authority to determine which of the Christian princes should be charged with the missionary enterprise, and that in the interests of peace and of the rapid furthering of the enterprise the Pope could also debar other Christian princes from taking part in it and from participating in the commerce arising from the religious mission.

In addition to the political interests that challenged the validity of the bulls, it must be remembered that religious controversy was raging throughout Europe, dividing it between Protestant partisans of reform and Catholics who defended the spiritual authority of the Pope. Among the latter group, Spain occupied an outstanding place. But let us not forget that some Catholic princes and authors were opposed to the temporal power of Rome.

We must not be surprised, then, that the true history of the bulls has suffered a great distortion. We may agree that intrinsically they did not differ from previous declarations of the Roman Curia with regard to similar questions. But the moment they were issued, the geographical immensity of the territory with which they dealt and the conflicting political and religious trends among European powers at the beginning of the modern age all contributed to make the case conspicuous and to make a historical understanding of it more difficult. The combined labor of modern investigators, although it may not have settled all doubts, has at least made possible a less impassioned interpretation of the bulls of Alexander VI.

· III ·

EVANGELICAL AND POLITICAL PROBLEMS OF PENETRATION IN THE NEW WORLD

We have already explained that the first patents justifying European penetration in the Indies, based upon the temporal sovereignty of the Pope or the world sovereignty of the Emperor, were criticized and restricted by authors belonging to the more advanced of the two schools of thought which, in a serious manner, dealt with the legal problems of America. Notwithstanding the paganism of the Indians, it was resolved that recognition should be accorded to their political rights since these proceeded from natural reason and human law and not from divine law or from grace. This more elaborate doctrinal statement of the American problem only complicated the search for titles which might validly unite Europe to the West Indies. The broadest powers in the Old World were no longer deemed sufficient. Nor was it considered admissible that the advance of the Europeans should rob the Indians of the fundamental rights of man, as was the case with enemy infidels.

What, then, were the titles that were later accepted as an adequate solution of the doctrinal problem of colonization?

One of the claims which contributed to that end was that of the Christian faith. Note that we speak of the religion of Christ and not of the temporal sovereignty of the Church, for, as already seen, the authors of the most advanced school of thought refused to admit its temporal sovereignty. However, such writers as Las Casas believed that the faith could be a just bond of relationship between Europeans and Americans since these writers regarded Christianity neither as a local phenomenon of the Occident nor as merely one religion that was compatible with others, but rather as the sole and universal means of salvation. All mankind living in sin could be redeemed only by receiving the one faith. Thus, when Europeans made ready to carry it abroad, they reasoned that they were offering to heathen an opportunity to escape damnation. In the opinion of Las Casas, therefore, the duty and the right to propagate the Christian faith among all men were incumbent upon the Pope.

Francisco de Vitoria favored, among several claims justifying colonization of the Indies, the right to universal intercourse by virtue of the *jus gentium*. He speaks of the brotherhood of mankind, of the original community of goods, the freedom of navigation, and of commerce between different peoples. Accordingly, such intercourse is not due simply to the arbitrary rule of human expediency but is protected by the *jus gentium* that unites all peoples. In line with these principles, he maintained that the Spaniards might send their ships wherever they wished without brooking interference, that they might settle in whatever country they pleased, and that both they and their children might become naturalized. But these rights did not necessarily imply sovereignty over the heathen, and Vitoria theoretically accepted as a satisfactory solution of this problem simple treaties of friendship and commerce, like those drawn up by the Portuguese with some of the African peoples.

Some authors believe that Vitoria was inspired by traditional Scholastic ideas regarding commerce between peoples. Others treat his argument as a forerunner of the commercial intercourse that has dominated modern times. Ignoring that question, one may well note that here, as in the case of the partisans of the foregoing claim based on the Christian faith, we encounter a European mind seeking in its particular field a universal formula to justify relationships between all peoples.

Another claim with the same characteristic of world-wide application was that founded on human reason. From the time of the Greeks this concept of reason had been one of the bases of political and moral philosophy; but how could it be used to solve the problem of colonizing America? We may recall that the rational Hellenic world was set apart by Greek writers from the barbarian world, which in the eyes of philosophers was both alien and irrational. Some Spanish thinkers of the sixteenth century were imbued with this same idea, which had reached its greatest development in Aristotle and had come to them either through Scholasticism or through the revival of classical learning in the Renaissance. To them, the European Christendom of their time corresponded to the rational civilization of Greece, and the people on the margin of the Christian world corresponded to the barbarians. The problem of contact between Spaniards and Indians could thus be regarded as a case of culture versus barbarism.

The consequence of this train of thought is obvious. As its most notable Spanish exponent, Ginés de Sepúlveda, would have expressed it: Because of the intellectual differences between Europeans and the aborigine of America, the latter should be subject to the former, and through this natural servitude he would improve his customs, exalting himself to true humanity, to virtue, and to religion.

The European imagined himself nearest of all men to the archetype of the species. He therefore considered himself chosen to extend his influence over other peoples, since all men should aspire to the dignity of a rational being.

To sum up: The faith, human reason, and intercourse in accordance with the *jus gentium* — these constituted the new values of which the most distinguished Spanish writers of treatises were thinking as a means of justifying European penetration in the West Indies. These claims of the revisionist school were rooted in the same European cultural tradition that inspired the older and more conservative writers who took a narrower view of the subject. The difference between these two schools of thought consisted in the fact that the claims of the revisionists were of broader scope and consequently more easily applicable to peoples outside the European world.

The relationships of which we have been speaking are obviously those between European and American men; for if the New World had been uninhabited, the right to the occupation of such lands (*res nullius* under Roman law) would have been sufficient to cover the case. The presence of human beings in America complicated the problem of finding a legal formula to govern the contacts between the peoples of two distinct worlds. It was therefore inevitable that many observations should be made and many theories enunciated regarding the nature of the primitive inhabitants of our continent.

We find the first data on this subject in the correspondence of Columbus immediately after the discovery. He describes with enthusiasm the beauties of nature in the West Indies and speaks of the inhabitants who go about naked and who enjoy a heavenly innocence. This idyllic tendency which took possession of the first European to visit the Antilles is found in many later writers. But Columbus was also a practical man of affairs, and in his travels through the islands he found other and very different Indians who ate human flesh and were extremely warlike. Those were the Caribs, with whom war promptly broke out and who were reduced to slavery by the Europeans. The discoverer of America wrote to the Catholic monarchs that the enslavement of these Indians might prove a source of wealth in the new lands.

As Spanish colonization spread through America, many Indian groups of varying cultures were discovered. Stories and opinions regarding their character were constantly arriving in Europe. Some were very unfavorable and others reflected the admiration shown in the passage written by Columbus.

Friar Tomás Ortiz speaks in 1525 of the great vices practised by the natives of the mainland, and he concludes that "God never created a people more sunk in vice and bestiality without any admixture of goodness or political discipline."

Ginés de Sepúlveda believed that the barbarians of the New World were as inferior to the Spaniards in prudence, ingenuity, virtue, and humanity as children are to adults, and women to men. The difference between them was as great as that between fierce and cruel persons and those who are merciful and humane; as between the intemperate and the temperate; and he was inclined to judge it as great as between monkeys and men.

On the other hand, Hernán Cortés, after observing the Aztec civilization, writes to his Emperor:

> I wish only to say that in their service and in conducting their affairs, they live almost as we do in Spain and with as much harmony and order as there, and considering that these people are barbarians, far removed from the knowledge of God and from communication with other rational nations, it is a wonder to see how rational they are in everything.

Years later, the Indians of New Spain appeared to Vasco de Quiroga, himself a choice spirit, as good, obedient, humble, fond of feasts and drinking, of pastimes and of nudity, like the people who lived in the days of the Kingdoms of Saturn. They enjoyed a great freedom of life and spirit and despised excess. In short, they were a living example of the Golden Age, which all the humanists of the time praised so highly.

Bartolomé de las Casas set against the naturalistic doctrine of Sepúlveda the Christian idea of the creation of man by God. Accordingly, all men are neighbors in the biblical sense, and they all have reasoning capacities and can be educated to a knowledge of culture and religion. He noted that the Indians lived in villages, which is an indication of reason, and that for the most part their bodies and members were well proportioned and their faces so good-looking that they seemed to be the children of lords.

It was not only in the field of observation and theory that the question arose of the nature of the American native. Theologians and jurists often met by official order during the sixteenth century to examine the problem, which was much debated because of its important relations to the type of government to be established for the Indians.

It is unnecessary to describe all these conferences, but we must mention one important consequence embodied in a bull of Pope Paul III in the year 1537. As is well known, it not only declared the Indians capable, as men, of receiving the faith of Christ but also that they embraced it with the greatest speed; that they were not and should not be deprived of their liberty or title to their property, and that they should not be reduced to slavery.

The Papacy thus adopted the liberal doctrine regarding the natives of America; and this position also triumphed in the disputes at the Spanish Court. In consequence, concepts of rational humanity and of liberty form the basis of the laws of the Indies.

The recognition of these principles involved another – that the Indians should enjoy complete liberty of will, and that the religious and political expansion of the Europeans should be carried forward only when it did not conflict with the wishes of the natives. To what extent did this doctrine influence the ideas and the acts of Spanish colonization in the New World?

Regarding acceptance of the faith, Christian writers did not forget that St. Thomas Aquinas and other learned men held the opinion that belief was conditioned upon free will. They also kept in mind the work of the first apostles of the Church which was carried out solely by the gentle means of convincing their hearers. Missionary work in the sixteenth century differed somewhat from that of the first apostles, since the Church was prominent in the European world and there were Catholic princes who placed the temporal forces of their states at the disposal of the religious enterprise. Was it permissible to combine political force with the missionary task of spreading the faith? Or should missions among the Indians be confined to preaching the Gospel, without temporal aid?

The partisans of a purely missionary labor admitted that

the faith must be offered to all men, but they conceded the right to accept or reject it. Rejection, although it was a sin, could not be punished in this world. So wrote Vitoria, Las Casas, and Domingo de Soto. The last named not only speaks of freedom to accept or reject the faith but also of freedom to hear it preached; he believed that the preachers could not force the heathen to hear the Gospel.

The more advanced Christian writers maintained that if the heathen refused baptism after hearing a peaceable explanation of the faith, the only proper thing to do was to leave them, without war or any show of force, since only God knew when and how they would be brought to the true religion.

Those of the opposite opinion, headed by Sepúlveda, were more sceptical. They thought that the missionaries of the sixteenth century lacked the perfect faith, the gift of miracles, and the knowledge of unknown tongues which enabled the first apostles to subdue the most impious of enemies. The only effective method of preaching the Gospel was to conquer the heathen by force of arms.

There were authors who, without admitting the need for previous conquest as a legitimate method of propagating the Christian faith, believed that once the pagans had been voluntarily brought under the jurisdiction of the Church they might be considered subjects of the King of Spain without any need for a separate expression of political will since the bulls of Pope Alexander VI had had that effect. Preceding the induction of heathen into a Christian congregation, the papal documents had only a potential force *in habitu.* But after the Indians accepted the faith, the jurisdictional right of the Church over them became actual and, by the same token, the grants made to the Spanish monarchs. Las Casas subscribed to this opinion, but there were some who reasoned that the acceptance of the faith was one thing and vassalage to the Crown another. The only just claim which the Crown could make was that all or most of the Indians wished to become its vassals by their own free will.

There were also some champions of the idea that it was necessary to establish Spanish political sovereignty over the Indians who accepted Christianity in order to insure their continued allegiance to the faith. In criticism of this theory, it was replied with some reason that it ignored the will of the natives in secular affairs and that the change of political sovereignty might be interpreted as a punishment which could not properly be imposed as a consequence of acceptance by the heathen of the Christian religion.

The foregoing explanations bring out the extent to which religious and political arguments were united in the legal thought of the period. However, the Aristotelian principle of natural servitude and the tenet of voluntary choice by the Indians both properly belong in the field of strictly political science. We might add to this group of ideas the thesis strenuously urged by some writers that the Aztecs and Incas themselves did not possess their lands by hereditary title but by conquest. The history of the growth of those great indigenous empires showed that they had been built up by despoiling other peoples through war. Hence, the Spaniards reasoned, they in turn might forcibly displace the ancient rulers.

Another doctrine that had enjoyed great prestige among Spanish political writers was also influential. This was, that rulers were under an obligation to watch over the well-being of the commonwealth; and if in place of doing so they gave preference to their own concerns, they became tyrants who might be deposed. Some even went to the length of defending the legitimacy of tyrannicide. As it was believed that the Indian kings and chieftains were tyrants who oppressed the people, it was held that the Spaniards could intervene on behalf of their vassals to free them from tyranny.

Finally, some authors particularly emphasized the alliances and pacts of submission negotiated by the Spanish captains and the Indian chieftains, by virtue of which the latter became vassals of the Spanish Crown. While still recognizing the arguments proceeding from a religious basis, we must therefore acknowledge the existence of a school of political thought expressing secular viewpoints regarding occupation of the Indies.

If we shift from the realm of ideas to the facts regarding the spread of religion and political power in the New World, we find in the first place that missionary activities sometimes followed the path of the Spanish warriors. Such is the case of the Franciscan friars who arrived in New Spain after the conquest achieved by Hernán Cortés. In other cases, the preacher preceded the soldier and went alone among the pagan Indians with the aim of converting them peacefully. Sometimes the missionaries suffered martyrdom. There were also some mixed enterprises in which the friars and the soldiers went forward together. The Spanish Crown accepted all these forms of missionary activity.

As for political penetration, at the beginning this was closely related to the wars of conquest, as we shall see in more detail in the next chapter. The Crown, however, always recommended that peaceful means of persuasion should be tried. There are some examples of negotiation between Spaniards and Indians. When Hernán Cortés first entered the city of Tenochtitlán, he succeeded in obtaining from Moctezuma a formal recognition of the overlordship of the King of Spain and the payment of a tribute amounting to six hundred thousand pesos.

Later on, Viceroy Antonio de Mendoza gathered together the leading Indian rulers and asked them to acknowledge anew their vassalage to the Spanish Crown, as this would justify the domination over them which had existed since the conquest by Cortés. He did this lest pretexts might be found which would obscure the validity of earlier claims. And as late as November 4, 1605, a document was signed at Valladolid by which the King of Spain bought from the descendants of Moctezuma "all the claims which they had or might have to the said empire [of Mexico], expressly renouncing them" in exchange for a pension, which was still being paid in 1820.

·IV·

THE DOCTRINE OF JUST WAR

DURING the period when the validity of the proclamation (requerimiento) drawn up by Palacios Rubios was admitted, and even after the first statement of the problem of Spanish claims to the West Indies had been revised, systematic consideration was given to the possibility that relations between the Europeans and the Indians might take the form of war. We should therefore pause to investigate the doctrine of war which then prevailed. In doing so, we shall see that the changes that have subsequently taken place in instruments and techniques of warfare have been accompanied by a corresponding change in the philosophy of war.

In pre-Christian treatises it is easy to find allusions to the valor of rulers, their glory, and their desire for power as incentives favoring belligerent procedure. But Christians are bound by a doctrine of peace in dealing with this problem. For Christians, could war ever be permissible, or would it always be contrary to Christian doctrine because it embodies force? This was one of the great problems of patristic philosophy.

In spite of Christianity, war continued to be fought and new views were shaped to fit this fact. Christian thinkers did not condemn all war; they merely demanded that it be just and for sufficient and reasonable cause. From the time of St. Augustine these thinkers also asked that the aim of war should be the reëstablishment of peace. These basic ideas continued to develop through the medieval period, and by the time we reach the *Summa Theologica* of St. Thomas Aquinas in the thirteenth century we find a mature Christian doctrine on the problem of war.

Scholastic doctrine demands, in the first place, that war be declared by a lawful authority, that is, an authority which is not subject to another sovereign power in temporal affairs; for if the dispute is one between subjects, they must refer it to a judge who is above them both, that he may decide the issue. War may be waged legitimately only when a quarrel affects sovereign powers who cannot have recourse to any higher authority to bring about the reëstablishment of justice. In the second place, it was held that the war must be for a just cause — that is, it might be waged if the enemy were at fault and in order to right a wrong done by him if peaceful means of reparation were refused. The third and final requirement was the upright intent of the party waging the war. His purpose must be to vindicate the wrongs done him by another and not to plunder or to inflict punishment entirely disproportionate to the extent of the injury suffered.

This theory of a just war prevailed in the universities of Europe at the time of the Conquest of America. If we examine the treatises of Vitoria, for example, we find allusions to all these principles. He maintains that only a grave wrong can justify war. Suárez says that the just cause must be absolute in character according to natural law; that is, that the rights of one of the parties shall have been violated or that the issue be that of defending innocent victims. This mention of the defense of the innocent was of considerable importance in the case of America, for it was claimed that a European power had the right to intervene to save the life of any persons, including children, who were destined for human sacrifice.

Even a glance at the development of ideas on the subject of war since the sixteenth century shows that they have greatly changed. War is no longer, as in medieval theory, a process of vindication based on reasons of justice or a means by which an aggrieved party seeks compensation for an injury done it. Of course, in the Middle Ages acts of war were not always in keeping with the prevailing doctrine. But in the modern period not only has this divorce between fact and theory continued but theory has more and more abandoned ideas of morality and justice. Thus a war is now justified on the ground that the growing power of a nation constitutes a threat, or because of commercial competition between nations, or for some other imperialistic motive. It is not for us here to make a special study of these modern ideas but only to point out that the Spanish Conquest of America is situated historically at the meeting point of medieval and modern doctrines, when *just* war – not merely war without qualification – was still spoken of and the facts were interpreted in the light of Scholastic theory.

As we have pointed out from the first, the international problem of the New World was considered in terms of the proper relationship between Christendom and pagan peoples. Hence, among the various types of war this is the one that merits our closest attention.

Let us briefly review the writings of some Spanish authors regarding wars waged by Christians upon infidels.

Palacios Rubios declared that when infidels did not recognize the superiority of the Church or refused to admit Christian preachers to their territories war might justly be waged against them. (We have already explained the bases of the idea relating to the temporal universal power of the Pope.) He then admitted other causes for war against infidels; for example, if they combatted the faith or harassed the Christians in particular ways, or blasphemed, or committed crimes of *lèse majesté*. For it is just to vanquish the infidel in order to free Christians from danger, not only when the former actually behave in any of the aforementioned ways but when there is a strong presumption that they may do so. By this latter example he referred especially to the continuous war which was fought by the Europeans against the Saracens, and which admitted of no truce. The Saracens were considered perpetual enemies, and in their case the rules of war came to be extremely rigorous. The same author thought that the heathen dwelling in Christian kingdoms may be expelled if it was feared that they might act against the Catholic faith. In this manner the expulsion of the Jews during the reign of the Catholic monarchs was justified. Finally, he admitted that infidels might be despoiled of lands that formerly belonged to Christians; the principal example of this being, of course, the Spanish reconquest against the Moors and the fall of Granada.

Gregorio López, who was a commentator on the laws of Castile and a member of the Council of the Indies, believed an injury to missionaries or merchants to be a primary cause for war. He also held that if infidels placed impediments in the way of peaceful life with their converted brothers, this constituted another legitimate reason for taking up arms. Let us suppose that some of the inhabitants of an Indian kingdom were converted, and that others began hostilities against them for this reason. According to López, there would then exist a just cause for war on the part of the Christians, who would aid the converted Indians against the oppressing infidel group. The author finally fell back upon the argument of human sacrifice which, in his opinion, made it lawful to use force to save innocent victims.

Bartolomé de las Casas considered war between Christian and infidels justified in three cases. First, if the latter should war upon and thus disturb Christendom, as in the case of the Saracens. Secondly, if they should maliciously persecute, disturb, or hinder the faith, whether by killing its adherents and preachers without legitimate cause, or by attempting to force those who had accepted the faith to renounce it, or by offering inducements to leave the Christian faith and accept their own. All this, according to Las Casas, comes under the head of hindering and persecuting the faith. And if the defense of temporal things is licit, how much more so must be the defense of spiritual things. In the third place, he considered the case of war against heathen in unjust possession of Christian lands or other Christian property. However, the entire philosophy of Las Casas is permeated by an evident pacifism. He declared that wars are a pestilential plague and a terrible calamity to mankind.

Ginés de Sepúlveda, although he belongs not to the group of theologians but rather to the political philosophers of the Italian Renaissance, not only thought that a just cause was necessary before undertaking a war, but also that it should be undertaken by legitimate authority only and with an upright mind, and should be conducted in an honorable manner. That is, he echoed the traditional theory of the Scholastics. But among the just causes of war which he enumerated (such as legitimate defense, the recovery of things unjustly taken away, and the imposition of merited punishment upon evildoers who have not been punished in their own city) he mentioned one cause which he himself conceded was less clear and less frequent, and which in fact formed no part of traditional Scholastic thought regarding war. This was "to subdue by force of arms, if no other means be possible, those who by their natural condition ought to obey others, but who refuse to accept their domination"; in other words, a war in behalf of a hierarchy supposedly justified by rational differences among men. The fact that the European, in the opinion of Sepúlveda, was superior to American heathen in the use of reason was sufficient to justify the forced subjugation of the latter to the domination of the former.

It may be asked whether such an inquiry as this does not lead us into juridical and theological abstractions without real significance and importance for American history. It has always been my opinion that an inquiry of this kind is indispensable to an understanding of the phenomenon of the Conquest. I shall present some reasons to justify this belief.

Let us examine the conduct of a warrior of some education like Hernán Cortés, and let us see whether in his acts we may not perceive the influence of Scholastic thought regarding war which prevailed among the writers of his time and country. In this way, we shall descend from the academic atmosphere to that of the men of action who were charged with establishing dominion over the Indians.

A law of the *Partidas* had declared that war ought to be a means toward peace, in accordance with the doctrine of St. Augustine. Just causes for war, according to the Spanish code, would be to expand the people's faith and to destroy those who wished to vex it; to fight for their lord, to the end of serving, honoring, and faithfully defending him; to protect themselves, and to increase and honor their own homeland.

When Hernán Cortés explained to his soldiers the causes of the war they had undertaken, he told them that for their part they had just motives and reasons:

> One, to fight for the increase of our holy faith and against barbarian people; another, to serve your Majesty; another, to safeguard our own lives; and for another, having many friends among the natives to aid us, this was a highly sufficient reason to lend courage to our hearts.

It is easy to see the resemblance between the text of the Spanish law and the discourse of the conqueror of Mexico. This suggests that a copy of the *Partidas* may have fallen into the hands of the soldiers, who were accustomed since the time of the Cid to know law as well as warfare.

The crusading character in defense of the faith which distinguished the enterprise of Cortés is emphasized in other documents, wherein he wrote to the Emperor that he encouraged his soldiers by telling them to remember that they were vassals of the King and that Spaniards had never been dismayed and were going to win the greatest kingdoms and fiefs then existing in the world, and that, in addition to doing what they were bound to do as Christians, "in fighting against the enemies of our faith," they would thereby gain glory in the next world and win the greatest renown and honor that any generation until that time had won in this world; that they must remember that they had God on their side and that nothing was impossible to him, as they might see from the victories they had won.

Elsewhere Cortés informed the King of an action favorable to the Spanish arms, saying: "As we carried the banner of the cross and battled for our faith and in the service of your holy Majesty in his very royal venture, God gave us so great a victory that we killed many people, without ourselves receiving any harm."

In his will this conquistador again spoke of having always received great honor and favor from the hand of God, as much in the victories he won against the enemies of the holy Catholic faith as in the pacification and settlement of the Indian kingdoms.

In some battles, the soldiers of the conquering armies claimed to have seen St. James the Apostle mounted on his white horse and fighting against the Indians, as they believed he had so often done in the wars against the Moors in Spain, because both were crusades in defense of the propagation of the faith.

In addition to the requirement of a just cause demanded by doctrine and the laws, one may observe among the conquerors of New Spain recognition of the requirement of honorable intention. In the military ordinances that Hernán Cortés drew up in Tlaxcala when he was making ready to return against Tenochtitlán, he charged his companions that

their principal motive and intention must be to dislodge and root out idolatry from all the natives of these regions and to bring them, or at least to desire to bring them, to salvation, and that they may be brought to a knowledge of God and of his holy Catholic faith; for if the said war were fought with any other intent, it would be unjust and everything taken in it would be obnoxious, and restitution would have to be made, and his Majesty would have no reason to order those who took part in such war to be rewarded. And I charge the consciences of the said Spaniards regarding it; and I now protest in the name of his Catholic Majesty that my principal intent and motive is to make this war and others that may be waged in order to bring and reduce the said natives to the said knowledge of our faith and belief, and later to subjugate them and bring them under the yoke and imperial and royal sovereignty of your holy Majesty, to whom the overlordship of all these regions belongs.

The requirement of legitimate authority did not worry Cortés, for he intended to carry out all his acts in the name of the King of Spain; and the difficulties which he had with the Governor of Cuba, Diego Velásquez, he endeavored to settle by means of the new power he had received from the municipal council (*cabildo*) established in Vera Cruz.

It seems reasonable to conclude that the legalistic atmosphere surrounding the actions of the conqueror of New Spain is not alien to the traditional principles of the Scholastic philosophy.

The evolution of ideas regarding the Conquest is reflected in the statutes which the Crown prepared as the military occupation of the continent proceeded.

As already explained, the proclamation of Palacios Rubios – the requerimiento – and the principles upon which it was based were accepted by the Spanish Crown as official doctrine for many years, and the conquests of Mexico and of Peru were carried out in accordance with them. Subsequently, however, criticisms of a theoretical nature began to influence the laws of the Conquest. The laws of Barcelona of 1542 restricted the war waged by the Spaniards against the Indians, and peaceful counsels regarding the nature of war predominated in the instructions given by the Crown to the captains.

A more advanced stage of this evolution is illustrated by the ordinances for pacification and settlement issued by Philip II in 1573, which not only recommended that the use of force be avoided in so far as possible but also forbade the use of the word "conquest" in official documents. The word "pacification" was to be substituted for it so that no doubt might exist regarding the intentions of the Spanish state.

Las Casas commented as follows on this change:

Even the Turks would not dare to speak of conquest and of placing people under the yoke of servitude, as was done by the Council of the Indies through the ignorance and blindness of its members, who were not aware that such words do not become any Christian king, least of all the King of Castile; they likewise ignored the differences between infidels [of the Old World], who oppose us, who are the enemies of our faith, and who have usurped our lands, and the Indians [of the New World], who live peacefully on their own lands and who owe nothing to the Christians or to the monarchs of Castile. These expressions were used for many years in the Council of the Indies, while the aforesaid blindness lasted, until the priest Bartolomé de las Casas, after many years showed to them their error.

Certainly Las Casas contributed to bringing about the change and he did not conceal his satisfaction over it, but other distinguished thinkers coöperated in this important reform.

When, years later, the Laws of the Indies were codified in 1680, it was possible to put an end to the evolutionary cycle by ordering, in Law 9, Title 4, Book III, "That war cannot and shall not be made on the Indians of any province to the end that they may receive the Holy Catholic faith or yield obedience to us, or for any other reason." This represented an attitude opposite to that of the proclamation which was valid during the first years of the American conquest. Violent means were no longer considered legitimate for realizing the religious or political purposes of European colonization. The code (*Recopilación*) of 1680 admitted only a few exceptions with regard to Indians such as the Caribs and the Araucanians, who had distinguished themselves by their violent opposition to the Spaniards and who created permanent war zones in the expansive empire.

The foregoing exposition warrants the conclusion that the Spanish Conquest, in which religious and political motives were intermingled, closed the medieval cycle of crusades. We have already seen that Cortés and his companions believed that they were fighting for the faith. Later, in the modern world, religion ceased to be a fundamental cause for the expansion of nations. But we have also seen that in the Spanish Conquest some political arguments were employed which open the chapter of modern imperialism. Among these were the distinction between superior and inferior beings and the justification of the dominion of civilized peoples over the natives of other lands — a relation which, it was held, might legitimately be established by force if necessary.

Many English, North American, and German authors are beginning now to study the Spanish Conquest as an early form of imperialism and a precursor of the great developments which have taken place in this field in the modern world down to our own day. But, without leaving the field of political doctrine, properly speaking, it must not be forgotten that even the most imperialistic of all the Spanish authors, Sepúlveda, justified the tutelary mission of the Europeans with the argument that it would elevate the aborigines to higher levels of human reason. In this way, imperialism was invested in his argument with an intimate sense of the perfectibility of men in political as well as in religious life. Later imperialisms have held that the civilizing mission consists rather in the communication of material benefits or have completely forgotten that they are under an obligation to confer any benefit at all upon subject peoples, at times even failing to preserve their lives on the ground that control over natural resources belongs to the strongest.

Spanish authors also went so far as to propound the contemporaneously burning international theme of "living room" (*Lebensraum*). In the treatise of Sepúlveda regarding war with the Indians, he asks:

> If a ruler, not through avarice, nor through thirst for empire, but through the narrowness of the boundaries of his state or its poverty, makes war upon his neighbors in order to take possession of their territories as an almost necessary step, will that constitute a just war?

The author promptly replies: "That would not be war but robbery."

Vitoria declared in his second "Lecture on the Indians" that "Neither is the enlargement of empire sufficient cause for making war." This appeared to him "too clear to need any demonstration." The same reason might be adduced by any belligerent. Neither, he held, is personal glorification of the ruler a just cause for war, nor any other personal advantage to him, for a ruler must order war as well as peace for the well-being of the nation. He may not employ the public revenues for his personal convenience or glory, and still less may he expose his subjects to danger. A good king is distinguished from a tyrant by the fact that the tyrant orders his government for the benefit of his own affairs and comfort and the true king orders it to the common well-being.

These quotations demonstrate the lack of sober judgment in the generally accepted affirmation that the claim of Spain to the Indies in the sixteenth century was the right of conquest conceded by the "ideas of the time." It is undoubtedly a matter clouded by confusion. The motive of expansion was not a just cause for war according to Scholastic doctrine. Spanish authors, not excepting Sepúlveda, did not admit the right of conquest for conquest's sake. On the other hand, when there was legitimate cause to declare war in accordance with their ideas, and when it was actually waged, they admitted among its just effects the possible domination of the conquered if the harm which the latter had done to the conqueror was sufficient to warrant such punishment.

· V ·

INDIAN SLAVERY

JUST war, interpreted as a vindication of injuries received by a sovereign power, leads to various economic consequences, for the offended power may collect from the conquered enemies the costs of the war and reparation for the damages and losses caused it by the injuries in question. Likewise, some margin is allowed for vengeance or punishment of the offenders.

In addition to the effects of war upon immovable property, such as the retention of lands, fortresses, cities, or kingdoms, the soldiers were also accustomed to take possession of movable booty and to enslave prisoners of war.

Spanish law on this question, so far as it related to booty and captives, had had a long development in the Peninsula and traditional rules and procedures had been established by the time the Conquest in America took place. The *Partidas* contain numerous precepts regarding the distribution of goods taken from the enemy. A relationship is established between what the soldiers carried or wore when they went off to the war and the distribution of prizes. So, if a man went as a common foot soldier he received less than if he was mounted. The minuteness of detail reached the point of enumerating the pieces of armor worn by each combatant. If it was complete to the hands, he received more than if his arm was not covered, and so on. In the division of spoils a greater portion was allotted to the captain who, according to the law of the *Partidas,* received a seventh of the spoils. First, however, a fifth of the spoils was set aside by law for the King as a royal perquisite.

In the wars against the Saracens, the rules relative to prisoners had acquired great rigor. The captives were sold into slavery, including the women and children. On the other hand, when the wars were between Christian rulers it was the custom to demand ransom of prisoners but not to condemn them to slavery.

From the time of St. Augustine it had been argued that the conqueror had the right to kill prisoners of war, but their lives might be spared in exchange for slavery.

The theoretical distinction which we have already noted between enemy infidels and heathen who were ignorant of the faith came likewise to have an influence upon the practical consequences of captivity. For if the Indians of America were comparable to the Saracens, the wars against the former would involve the legal consequence of slavery and the sale of the conquered without sparing the women and children, as the requerimiento drawn up by Palacios Rubios made clear. But if it was believed that the Indians belonged to the type of heathen who had never heard of the faith, the policy toward them could be more merciful.

As regards the system of distributing captives, the practice of direct seizure prevailed in some wars, so that the soldier who took a prisoner on the field of battle could keep him and sell him. In most cases, however, captured prisoners were gathered in one place, and under the supervision of the commanding officer they were distributed among the captains and the soldiers according to the merit and rank of each. The prisoners might also be sold at auction and the profits, not the prisoners themselves, be distributed. In the distribution of prisoners the usual perquisite of the royal fifth was collected.

Let us now inquire how the problem of dealing with captives was worked out in the first wars waged by the Spaniards against the American Indians. In the first place, there existed an important precedent set up by the conquest of the Canary Islands. In these isles the Spaniards encountered an important native population with whom they established relations that included incidents of enslavement, and these were primarily a consequence of the war.

The same phenomenon occurred in the colonization of the Antilles. If we follow the steps of Cortés during his conquest of New Spain, we find that after the *Noche Triste*,[1] when he conducted his second campaign against the Aztec capital, he decreed slavery for many Indians, among them women and children. In the expeditions of Pedro de Alvarado to the south, the same thing occurred. The Governor of Pánuco, Nuño de Guzmán, shipped great numbers of Indian slaves to the West Indies. The merchants who bought them and carried them to the islands were obliged to furnish bond to bring horses, livestock, and implements of labor to Mexico in exchange for the slaves. In his reports to the King, the energetic Governor boasted that by this means the Spanish settlers were provided with what they needed, and that prior to his administration one hundred slaves used to be given in exchange for one horse but that later, as a result of his measures, the exchange became fifteen slaves for a horse or mare. Nuño de Guzmán was later promoted to the presidency of the first *Audiencia*[2] of Mexico and continued to favor the policy of enslavement. The same thing occurred during his conquest of New Galicia.

In the year 1531 the Opilcingo Indians rebelled. Cortés sent Captain Vasco de Porcallo against them, and he took from one to two thousand slaves. In 1541 the great revolt of the Indians of New Galicia occurred. With the consent of the Audiencia, Viceroy Mendoza declared war to the death, with slavery as a consequence. After many violent battles, in which Mendoza was present and Pedro de Alvarado lost his life, the ringleaders of the Indians were put to death and other Indians were distributed as prisoners of war in the presence of the commanding officer, the captains receiving a proportion-

1 That is, the disastrous retreat of the Spaniards from the rebellious city of Tenochtitlán, June 30, 1520.

2 The *Audiencia* was primarily a judicial body, though it had other functions as well. It was the highest court of appeal in the colonies.

ately larger number and the soldiers whatever corresponded to their rank and merit. In such ways the war in New Spain in the first half of the sixteenth century yielded a considerable number of Indian slaves.

Meanwhile, another cause of slavery which the Spaniards called *rescate* (barter) had come into effect. This consisted of deals by means of which Indians were obtained from the chiefs who kept slaves in accordance with the rules of paganism. The Spaniards intended them for the mines, the farms, herding, and so on. In support of this traffic, they argued that the Indians passed into the control of Christians who could teach them the faith and rescue them from sacrifice at the hands of Indian priests. Indeed, if the pre-Hispanic law of slavery in Mexico is studied, one finds that there were certain slaves, of whom Sahagún speaks at length, called "the fattened" or "the washed" and who were selected for sacrifice. In the great festivals of the merchants they were devoured after their hearts had been offered to the gods. This strange type of men were seen by the Spaniards when the armies of Hernán Cortés left Vera Cruz for Tenochtitlán. Bernal Díaz relates that they opened the cages in which the Indians were kept awaiting the moment of sacrifice.

In addition to war and barter, the Spaniards availed themselves of another means of obtaining slaves from the chieftains. This consisted of receiving them in lieu of the *encomienda*[1] tribute. Generally this tribute was paid in gold or in natural or industrial products; but when the chief could not pay the Spaniard the required amount in gold he was accustomed to substitute a number of men or women slaves.

Indian misdemeanors might also be a cause for perpetual slavery or for servitude for a number of years. The Indians could not easily adapt themselves to Spanish laws and customs, and they committed offenses which according to European criteria merited severe punishment, including the death penalty. Spanish colonial magistrates understood that the ap-

[1] Groups of Indians apportioned by the Crown to Spanish individuals.

plication of their own criteria would result in excessive rigor in administering justice, and they obtained from the Crown permission to commute death sentences to perpetual or temporary slavery. The criminal branch of the Audiencia of Mexico generally heard cases of this kind. The convicted criminals were sold to the workshops or other labor establishments.

During the first period of Spanish colonization the Crown did not openly oppose the development of Indian slavery; it demanded merely that the facts should satisfy the laws promulgated to cover each method of acquiring slaves.

With regard to enslavement through war, following the requerimiento or proclamation whose contents and operation we have already observed, the Crown continued to admit the possibility that conquered Indians might be reduced to servitude. In the instructions sent by Charles V to Hernán Cortés in 1523, the Emperor recommended that when the Spaniards demanded that the Indians submit peacefully to the sovereignty of Spain they should give the natives to understand, through interpreters, the benefit to be derived from it and the evil, harm, and death which would be their lot if they opposed it. The Indians were particularly warned that those who were taken alive would be enslaved. But the Emperor also cautioned Cortés that the Christians would greatly prefer that the Indians should go to war instead of accepting peace in order to provide a pretext for enslaving them, and he directed Cortés to bear this in mind in considering the testimony of Christians in such cases.

In the ordinances of Granada of 1526 and those of Toledo in 1528, although it was required that wars be undertaken justly and captives seized legitimately, it was still admitted that slavery might be the penalty for Indians who resisted submission to the Spaniards.

The conquistadors of Mexico requested the authorities of the island of Hispaniola for official permission to barter slaves with the chieftains. When they sent their first solicitors to Spain they ordered them to procure royal authorization for such contracts. The Crown issued an edict, October 15, 1522, granting the desired authorization.

The barter of slaves created very delicate problems. Chieftains decreed the servitude of the Indians in accordance with the norms and customs of pre-Hispanic law; but when the slaves were transferred into the hands of the Spaniards, they came under the operation of European law. However, neither the causes of slavery nor the juridical status of slaves were identical under the two systems.

Investigations into the grounds for enslavement in Indian law have shown that the reasons were often trifling and without validity under the principles of Spanish jurists. One slave told the treasurer of New Spain, Albornoz, that he had wished to make use of another Indian's kettledrum (*tabal*) and the latter was thus enabled to enslave him. Hunger or petty theft also led to enslavement.

The doctrines of Roman law and those of the Spanish law required in these cases a thoroughgoing review of the origins of slavery, with the aim of eliminating slight or unjust causes. Hence, in this sense European law came to exercise a moderating influence upon the heathen law, and one favorable to human freedom. Pre-Hispanic law also permitted the sacrifice of men and women slaves in religious ceremonies, as we have seen. In some cases the victims were children. This custom could not be tolerated under principles of European culture, and the slave who passed by barter from the hands of his Indian masters to those of the Spaniards was freed from that mortal threat.

The moderating and liberal influences of European law should not, however, lead us to forget that in other respects the condition of the Indian became worse when the European system of slavery was imposed upon him, for the labor he had been obliged to perform under pre-Hispanic slavery was apparently less heavy than that demanded by his new Spanish master. The slaves of the pagan regime might have certain possessions, a small house, and although they had to serve the master when he summoned them they did not have to serve him constantly. Moreover, the children of the Indian slaves could be free, while according to European law the child born of a slave was also a slave.

The application of Indian and Spanish law to this problem of slavery revealed such interesting variations that during the administration of the Second Audiencia of New Spain, the *oidor* (judge of the Audiencia), Vasco de Quiroga, was designated to hear cases relating to Indian slaves in his division of the court. He decided to associate with him four of the highest of the native judges so that they might explain to him the use and custom in each case. The Spanish judge listened to their opinions, and if they appeared reasonable and in accordance with Christian ideas he admitted them. If not, he modified or rejected them.

It is a demonstration of the flexibility of the law of the conquering people that, essentially, it allowed the law of the conquered people to control the barter or ransoming of slaves between Spaniards and Indians without thereby debarring the revision of customs that were barbarous and inacceptable to European culture.

This attitude was not maintained merely with respect to slaves. That was a matter in which the conqueror might be suspected of having an interest in retaining the foundations of pagan slavery. But the same attitude prevailed with respect to the choice of Indian chieftains and the rule governing the inheritance of that office, with respect to the tributes owed by the vassals to their former lords, with respect to lawsuits, and so on. Accordingly, Law 4, Title 1, Book II, of the Laws of the Indies provided:

> We ordain and command that the good laws and customs which the Indians formerly had for their good government and order, and the usages and customs which they have retained since they became Christians that are not opposed to our holy religion nor to the laws of this book, and those which have later been made and ordained may be retained and enforced; and we hereby approve and confirm this, if necessary, by these presents, subject to such additions as may appear to us desirable.

This spirit of accommodation was not peculiar to the Laws of the Indies but was found also in the law of the Spanish Peninsula. In Seville were gathered many Negroes who were difficult to govern. The King ordered that one of them should be recognized by the Spanish authorities as leader by virtue of the fact that it was said he was a noble and knew the usages and customs of those inhabitants. In this case the juridical entity of the foreign people was not yet established, but the King proceeded to create it in order to facilitate government of the group and their relations with Spanish law.

Years earlier, the Spain of the Cid was broken up into several Christian and Moorish kingdoms which made war on one another but also at times had peaceful relations among themselves and with the groups of Jews who were established in their territories. If to these historical precedents we add the sense of organic order that prevailed in medieval law, we can easily understand the flexibility of Spanish institutions at the beginning of the modern period.

As enslavement of the Indians developed in New Spain, voices were raised in opposition to it and in defense of the freedom of the natives. The noble pleas of Zumárraga, Vasco de Quiroga, the Franciscans of Guatemala, Las Casas, and others have come down to us. The presence of these men who sponsored the initiation of humanitarian practices is continuous in the history of Spanish institutions in America and constitutes a reforming force whose study cannot be omitted.

Their anxiety first showed itself in the sphere of doctrine, but they had an influence upon the royal councils and later upon the laws passed to regulate relations between Spaniards and Indians. In opposition to this liberal thought stood the interests of the colonists, who tried by every means to increase exploitation of the natives and who made their voices heard through solicitors to the Court. They represented the realism and the materialism of colonization. Legal institutions developed amid these forces, and their historical evolution often reflects the incidents of the struggle.

The liberal thought of that period was no accidental

growth; on the contrary, it formed an organic part of the state and of the life of Spain. It sprang from a theological and philosophical construction which presupposed the creation of man by God, the brotherhood which should unite all men as neighbors in the biblical sense, and the natural rights held by a man in himself and in his social life. Government was conceived as an institution for the well-being of the commonwealth, and a Christian ruler was expected to scrutinize his acts according to the higher norms of his conscience and of the divine and natural law which were over him. His counsellors were under obligation to advise him in serious cases for the good of the kingdom and in accordance with the spiritual duties resting upon the ruler. All his subjects, especially those belonging to religious orders, considered themselves bound to give whatever information and advice they deemed suitable on questions of policy, or to remind him of the principles which seemed pertinent. Therefore, high magistrates and prelates as well as humble friars and settlers wrote to the king regarding matters of Indian rule, and at times so did the Indians themselves. Amid that chorus of voices, learned or simple, interested or altruistic, those of men liberally inspired by Christianity and philanthropy were conspicuous as representing a permanent and active aspiration toward principles of justice.

In the protest that was raised against the enslavement of the Indians, it was claimed that the wars undertaken by the Spaniards were unjust and could not properly result in captivity. Moreover, the conquistadors failed to respect the instructions given them by their monarchs. With regard to the system of barter, it was pointed out that the original causes of pre-Hispanic slavery were unjust and that this fact was sufficient to destroy the validity of the title by which the Spaniards acquired slaves held under pagan law, even though they were acquired by purchase or gift or as a form of tribute.

It is true that the Indians warred among themselves and as a result of such warfare they might seize captives in order, in their turn, to trade them to the Spaniards. But in reply it was stated that since they were people deprived of the Christian religion they had been unable to distinguish clearly what were just causes for war, and that the majority of them, at least in New Spain, made war for the purpose of capturing prisoners for sacrifice. Finally, it was argued that the inquests made by the Spanish authorities as a preliminary to incorporation of the pre-Hispanic slaves into the Spanish system betrayed serious carelessness and bad faith, so that many free Indians were branded and marked as slaves to the Spaniards.

In consequence of these protests great changes resulted in Spanish legislation relating to Indian slaves. These changes will be discussed in the next chapter.

·VI·

THE EMANCIPATION OF THE INDIAN SLAVES

A CEDULA of August 2, 1530, reveals clearly the impact upon Spanish colonial legislation of the movement in favor of abolishing Indian slavery. It explains that at the beginning of the discoveries the monarchs permitted the waging of war and the capture of Indians who forcibly resisted the King and who refused to acknowledge the Christian faith. Charles V himself authorized the enslavement of captives "as a practice which, through the rights and laws of our kingdom, could be done and permitted without burdening our conscience"; but in consideration of the many intolerable wrongs and the boundless avarice of the conquistadors, it was now commanded that henceforth no one should dare enslave such Indians in time of war, even though the war might be just and ordained by the King or by his vicegerent. It was also forbidden to acquire slave Indians through barter.

A census of slaves held prior to the date of the decree was to be taken under the supervision of the Audiencia. In this way the Indians already enslaved could be identified; and as the future reduction of Indians to slavery was forbidden, it might be expected that the institution would soon come to an end.

Hardly had the Audiencia published the decree in New Spain and begun to apply it when the soldiers and the settlers protested against it. The cabildos of the Spanish cities regularly supported these complaints.

The colonists argued that they were being deprived of a

right permitted by law and that the prohibition of enslavement would result in the death of more prisoners in war, since the soldiers would no longer have an interest in taking them alive. The majority of the expeditions to the Indies had been financed not by the state but by private capital, the captains and soldiers bearing the expense of the enterprise. And if the expeditionaries provided their own arms, horses, and supplies and paid for their medical treatment, what would it all profit them if the Crown prevented enslaving prisoners for the purpose of using them as such or of selling them?

With regard to barter, they argued that Indian slaves thus obtained by the Spaniards from the *caciques* (chieftains) were converted to the Christian faith and abandoned their barbarian customs.

These considerations did not fail to impress the Spanish Crown and in 1534 another cedula was issued, revoking the one of 1530 and again permitting the enslavement of the Indians in warfare and through barter; but women, and children under fourteen years at the time of their enslavement, could not legally be held in slavery. In the wars undertaken against the Saracens and other infidel enemies, as we have already seen, the enslavement of women and children as well as men was permitted; and the same was true of the first wars in America. Now, the law of enslavement with regard to the heathen of the Indies was more merciful, and this demonstrates that the distinction between various types of infidel, of which Cajetan and other writers of treatises had spoken, was beginning to be officially recognized.

The new order favoring slavery had hardly reached Mexico when jurists and members of the religious orders who had already protested against that institution renewed their protests to the Throne against it; and again the authorities at home yielded to the pressure of the abolitionists. The New Laws promulgated in Barcelona in 1542 provided that there was to be no future enslavement for any cause whatsoever; persons already enslaved might remain so but their cases were to be reviewed, and if their owners could not show a legal title to them the Indians were to be set free.

Let us make a general observation here with respect to the fluctuations that we have noted in colonial legislation. These are conspicuous in the matter of slavery and may also be discerned in the official attitude toward the problem of conquest. The theoretical and practical factors that determined them are clear when one notes the pressure group that originated the petitions which finally influenced a given law. These frequent and explicable changes demonstrate that the only method that can lead to an understanding of the historical development of colonial institutions is the one that follows them step by step and keeps in mind all the factors affecting the process. On the other hand, if we confine our study to the Laws of the Indies of 1680, we run the risk of considering only the final conclusions then reached by the official mind without achieving a vision of the preceding stages of their evolution. The jurists charged with drawing up a code of laws for the governance of the Indies naturally took care in so far as possible to avoid all contradictions. They did not undertake to write a history of colonial law but rather to organize legislation in a coherent code.

Returning to the theme of slavery, we find that the New Laws raised several problems of interpretation. Was it possible to adduce the proof they required of legitimate possession of the slave? If not, all the slaves would regain their liberty. In the second place, it had to be decided on whom the burden of proof was to fall. Would the slave have to demonstrate that he was a freeman and that he was illegally enslaved? Or would the master have to prove that he was justly in possession of the Indian under a legal title?

It was not easy to solve this aggregate of doubts. In 1546 important conferences of theologians and jurists were called in Mexico to discuss the interpretation of the New Laws of 1542. Las Casas defended the radical position. According to him, all the slaves, or at least the great majority of them, had been wrongfully taken, and he understood that the King's will in promulgating the New Laws had been to grant liberty to all of them. Other jurists believed that this was neither the spirit nor the letter of the ordinances, and that their true intent was to require a review of all cases of enslavement through war and barter, to free those who had been enslaved unjustly, and to leave in servitude those who had been enslaved in accordance with the law.

On February 20, 1548, the Crown explained that all women, and all children who were under fourteen years of age at the time they became slaves, were to be manumitted, without exception. As for males over fourteen, the owner must prove that the Indian had been taken in just warfare and that all the legal requirements had been met. In the case of Indians obtained otherwise than in war, the laws of the realm and the New Laws of 1542 were to be observed.

This declaration, inspired by the principle that there exists a presumption of liberty for all men, clearly placed the burden of proof upon the masters. Note also that it demanded, in addition to a title of seizure during war, that the war itself should have been conducted in accordance with the legal rules. This was an extremely difficult fact to prove when the issue involved wars that had occurred many years previously and when the witnesses might have died or might not be available. This explains why many masters, instead of trying to justify their titles, preferred to set their slaves free and merely tried to collect the price they had paid for them from the persons who had sold them.

The declaration relating to bartered Indians is somewhat vague, but beginning with December 1538 measures had been taken to prevent the chiefs from declaring the common Indians slaves. As a result, the traffic favoring the Spaniards sustained a heavy blow at its source.

The Crown's interest in abolition again appeared when it charged the Audiencias of the Indies to appoint solicitors to seek judicial means of emancipating the Indians, for it was feared that if the initiative were left to the natives they would not easily obtain reviews of their cases. The attorney Melgarejo was designated for this task in Mexico in 1551. After taking office, he wrote the Crown asking it to state definitively whether or not any slaves had been legally taken in the Indies. He stated that in the opinion of the Audiencias of Hispaniola and Guatemala the proof required by the New Laws was so difficult, if not impossible, to obtain that it was clearly the intent of these laws to free all the Indians, which was accordingly done. In New Spain, on the other hand, the idea prevailed among the judges that in some cases the Indians might have been justly enslaved, and Melgarejo himself was of this opinion. Consequently, instead of decreeing general emancipation the Audiencia undertook to review each case individually.

The movement toward emancipation was at first very slow in Mexico; but when it was noted that the Crown leaned increasingly toward a doctrine favorable to general emancipation, judgment of the cases began to manifest greater despatch and liberality. A royal cedula was received which ordered the emancipation of all slaves taken by Hernán Cortés in the conquest of Mexico. Finally the most formal and solemn war which had been fought in New Spain — the war against the Indian rebels of New Galicia during the time of Viceroy Mendoza — was not excepted from review, and the Indians captured in the course of it were declared free.

The process of emancipation lasted several years. The last Indian slaves appeared before the Audiencia in the year 1561; and as the Emperor had ordered Melgarejo to send him annual reports on the cases decided, we fortunately possess statistics on the subject, and these show that some three thousand slaves were liberated in Mexico. To these must be added those who were emancipated by the commissioners (*visitadores*) sent to the provinces, for the attorney Lebrón de Quiñones freed some six hundred slaves in Colima. In Guatemala the attorney Cerrato also labored with energy. The Crown's desire for emancipation was carried out in other Audiencias of the Indies as well, for the laws of which we speak were promulgated not merely for New Spain but for the Indies in general.

It is interesting to compare the figures shown in the documents with those given by the best-known histories of the colonial period, for there are authors who state that in the time of Viceroy Velasco one hundred and fifty thousand Indians were emancipated in a single year, whereas we have seen that in the course of ten years the numbers liberated reached three thousand in the Audiencia of Mexico.

The history of the Indies is full of disputed points, and statistics which appear therein are likely to be magnified in accordance with the emotions of each writer; but they are susceptible of a considerable downward revision by a critical study of documentary sources.

After the significant episode just reviewed, the doctrine of freedom prevailed in official circles in both Spain and the colonies. When the code of 1680 was promulgated, a law was inserted containing a general prohibition of slavery in peace or war, except in the case of Indians who carried on perpetual warfare against the Spaniards. These groups, such as the Caribs, the Araucanians, and the Mindanaos, were mentioned in special laws incorporated in the same code (Law 1, Title 2, Book VI, and Laws 12, 13, 14, and 16 of the same title and book).

Another important consequence of the emancipation of the Indians was the influence it had upon the problem of the Negroes. In the middle of the sixteenth century, when the humanitarian current of thought put an end to the enslavement of the natives of America, the introduction of African Negroes increased, and some authors began to ask themselves if the doctrine of freedom should not be extended to them, too. The Negroes were God's children like the Indians, and the wars and traffic by means of which the Europeans obtained them on the African coasts were characterized by injustices very similar to those that motivated the emancipation legislation just applied to the Indians in the colonial Audiencias.

This liberal current of thought was sustained by various Spanish authors. Las Casas had once pleaded for the substitution of Negro for Indian labor, but he not only later changed his opinion but also spoke of the injustices with which the Portuguese seized and enslaved the Africans. He held that the Negroes had been unjustly and tyrannically enslaved, "for the same reasoning applies to them as to the Indians." The Archbishop of Mexico, Friar Alonso de Montúfar, wrote the King on June 30, 1560: "We do not know for what reason the Negroes are captured any more than the Indians, for the Negroes, so they say, receive the Holy Gospel with good will and do not make war on the Christians." Friar Tomás Mercado called attention in 1569 to the cruelty and injustice of the European treatment of the Africans. Bartolomé de Albornoz stated in 1573 that the miserable Ethiopians were blameless and had done nothing to justify losing their freedom, and that no public or private claim was sufficient to absolve from blame those who held them in bondage.

This movement anticipated by two centuries the anti-slavery movement of the eighteenth-century Enlightenment; but it did not prosper in a Spanish environment and was overborne by the utilitarian current in favor of the African slave trade.

We must now ask ourselves if the mid sixteenth-century emancipation really put an end to Indian slavery in New Spain. We speak of slavery in the strict legal sense of the term, that is, of the Roman and European legal institution that granted one man the right to hold and dispose of another as property. We do not refer to mistreatment in general, or to institutions which, while they might limit somewhat the freedom of the Indian, did not reduce him to the status of legal servitude.

A very few years after the process of emancipation was completed in the Audiencia of Mexico, incessant warfare broke out between the Spaniards and the barbarian Indians of the north, who bore the name of Chichimecas. Viceroy Martín Enríquez called a conference (*junta*) in 1569 to study the legal problem of prisoners taken in that war. It was to be decided whether they were free in spite of the fact that they had attacked the Spaniards, or whether they could be enslaved notwithstanding the fact that emancipation had recently been granted the Indians in the center of the viceroyalty and that the laws forbidding enslavement were still in force. A compromise solution was adopted, which consisted in granting the soldiers the services of the Chichimecas for a period of ten years but excepted the women and children from slavery. In consequence of this ruling, Chichimeca prisoners began to appear in the central cities of the viceroyalty and were found working even in the Cathedral of Mexico City. They were sold and auctioned, and these transactions were registered in the notaries' books. At times women as well as men were held and transferred in this way – a fact which reveals that the law was becoming more rigorous.

This new form of slavery passed through alternating periods of approval and disapproval by the authorities, as had occurred with respect to the Indians captured in the first wars conducted by the Spaniards in America. From 1585 to 1588 Viceroy Villamanrique was distinguished by his zeal for the emancipation of the Chichimecas, who were still being captured on the frontiers and who had been sold in the most populous and industrious cities, such as Puebla. Nevertheless, the wars still continued, and so did the capture of the northern Indians and their sale as slaves by the Spaniards. A strong abolitionist movement began in the Audiencia of Guadalajara in 1672 and was supported by new Crown laws; but hostilities did not cease, and in the vast and poorly guarded northern provinces the germs of slavery reappeared. This was observed especially in the relations of the Spaniards of New Mexico with the Apaches. In the colony of Nuevo Santander, it was discovered in 1772 that along the banks of the Rio Grande the colonists were invading the Indian country in search of slaves, especially children, whom they later sold for various kinds of labor. The previous measures favoring emancipation had not been forgotten, however, and the higher authorities sought to repress this traffic.

The cruelty of the war with the intractable northern Indians led the viceregal government to permit prisoners to be taken out of the provinces, to be bound with halters or ropes, and to be brought to the capital city where they were lodged in the building of the *Acordada*. Later they continued toward Vera Cruz, where some were distributed among planters growing tobacco and others were shipped to Havana for work on the fortifications. The Mecos and Apaches who were thus transported often escaped and returned to the north, marking their route with murders and robberies.

The establishment of Mexican independence in the third decade of the nineteenth century did not put an end to the war against the border Indians. The newspapers of Chihuahua and other states in the new republic continued to publish items concerning attacks and harsh punishments. And the war against the Yaquis during the administration of Porfirio Díaz led to the revival of the practice of deportation which had been in use at the end of the colonial period.

These facts give a special character to the history of northern Mexico, and differentiate it from the colonization of the central area where the adjustment of indigenous and Spanish culture was brought about with less difficulty after the Conquest. In the former case, nomad and barbarian Indians were being dealt with. In the latter case, there were dense nuclei of Indian population upon which the institutions of the Spaniards devolved. War and enslavement persisted long on the frontiers, while they disappeared in the central regions, to be replaced by less onerous forms of relationships. However, where the Spaniards encountered somewhat settled people, as in New Mexico, the normal type of Hispano-Indian society was again reproduced. That province illustrates both the pacific relationship between the Pueblo Indians and the Spaniards — save during the periods of rebellion — and the hostility and enslavement in the case of the Apaches.

The pattern of frontier civilization, as distinct from that of the more populous regions, was repeated in other Spanish regions, for example those of Chile and the River Plate. Thus it may be stated that Spanish colonization in America does not present a single type, but several; and that this did not depend exclusively upon the will or the initiative of the colonists, but upon the conditions of the soil and of the type of native with whom they established relations. In every case, the colonizing culture brought with it homogeneous elements and tendencies of government toward the establishment of uniformity; but because of social realities this was not always attained.

In the Spanish frontier regions, situations arose bearing a certain similarity to those which were observed when the French or English cultures came in contact with barbarian Indians. To be sure, the methods and ideas of colonization varied from one European power to another; but some common features can also be distinguished, especially when the contact was with the same tribe, for example, the Apache. The bitter hostility which existed between Spaniard and Apache in northern Mexico was duplicated when the Anglo-Saxon colonists were attacked by the same Indians, who killed men and male children and enslaved women, some of whom have written in their diaries of the sufferings they had to endure.

Indian slavery in the hands of the Anglo-Americans is a broad theme which has been the subject of a competent monograph by A. W. Lauber.[1] Only when the history of that institution in the Spanish, Portuguese,[2] and French colonies in America has been written, will it be possible to make valid comparisons between them. This will open a new phase in the study of the institutional history of America, which will take the place of vague talk about similarities and differences and of hasty moral judgments that lack the support of historical knowledge.

[1] See Bibliography.

[2] Indian slavery in sixteenth-century Brazil has been the subject of a recent monograph by Dr. Alexander Marchant. See Bibliography.

· VII ·

THE ENCOMIENDA AS A POLITICAL INSTITUTION

As is well known, the Conquest of America was accomplished not by the armies of the Crown but through contracts made with individuals, in which it was stipulated that the members of the expedition should themselves bear the expense of the undertaking.

This system had already been employed in the conquest of the Canary Islands. One ancient chronicle states that Fernández de Lugo, one of the most important commanders, lacking the funds to organize an enterprise, went to the steps of the Cathedral of Seville where an angel rained down upon him all the gold he needed. The recent investigations of Wölfel have shown that Lugo entered into a contract with a group of merchants in order to obtain the necessary resources and Wölfel accordingly entitled his article: "Alonso de Lugo and Co., a Commercial Society for the Conquest of the Island of La Palma."

The conquistadors of America employed the same system. For example, the expedition of Cortés to New Spain was based upon private contributions as was pointed out in my study entitled *Private Interests in the Conquest of New Spain,* which was written from a point of view very similar to that of Wölfel's study of the history of the Canary Islands.

The private nature of these expeditions explains why those who took part in them expected remuneration in return for their expenses and their labor. Movable goods and captives constituted only a part of their remuneration, however, for the soldiers sought something else of a more permanent character.

They knew that in medieval Europe the most valiant warriors were raised after battle to the ranks of the nobility, becoming feudal lords with vassals. They believed that they themselves were entitled to similar rewards. Bernal Díaz echoed in this matter the collective sentiment of the American conquistadors. They were of high birth to begin with, he said, since they belonged to the class of hidalgos, and some were knights; and now their great deeds had added to the lustre of their names. Warriors of old had received from their kings villas, castles, and broad acres, as well as the appropriate privileges and exemptions. This had been done in the wars of King James of Aragon, in the conquest of Granada, in the expedition of the Gran Capitán, Gonzalo de Córdoba, against Naples, and in the days of the Prince of Orange. In like manner, said Bernal Díaz, should the deeds of the conquistadors be weighed in the balance, their achievements would be found worthy of rewards equal to those accorded the aforementioned knights of European fame.

These pretensions of the conquistadors to titles of nobility were supported by some jurists and members of the clergy. In his *Política de Corregidores y Señores,* Castillo de Bobadilla contended that during the reconquest of Spain from the Moors the Spanish monarchs "with their accustomed magnanimity and liberality, and in recognition of the great services performed in their behalf in smiting the enemy with all courage and strength, divided [among their men] the cities, towns, and places"; that the vassals thus raised to the nobility were the king's vicars, "the bone and sinew of the State, without whom it would be a boneless, nerveless mass of pulp and flesh."

Solórzano Pereira cited examples of the distribution of stipendiary or tributary land by the Romans. These tracts were called borderlands because they served as buffers along the frontiers. He reminds us also of the feudal fiefs of Germany, Lombardy, and Naples, as well as of the Spanish noble houses that traced their origin from the Moorish wars. Solórzano argued, therefore, that fiefs of the same kind ought to be established in the Indies, for they would be "like the bones and nervous system of the Commonwealth, and the lack of them would be a peril of the state."

Among the opinions expressed by the clergy of New Spain, that of the Dominican Domingo de Betanzos stands out because of its feudal point of view. About the year 1541 he wrote that if the Indians were placed directly under the lordship of the King instead of being given in encomiendas to the Spaniards, all the colonists of the Indies would be on the same level and all equal in their poverty, which was directly contrary to the tenets of good policy.

For it is necessary, in order that the commonwealth may be well ordered and well nourished, that it shall contain persons who are valiant, powerful, and rich, and knights and nobles, for these are the bones that sustain the commonwealth. For there can be no more unfortunate or miserable commonwealth than that in which all are poor and miserable and needy, for such as these can do nothing either to forward the commonwealth or to lend help one to another. Thus would it be if no one might hold either villa or domain, which would be highly undesirable aside from many other evils of which others can speak in further support hereof.

In a collective opinion given by the Dominicans in 1544, this medieval view of society was again described. The friars maintained that

in a well-ordered commonwealth, it is necessary that there be rich men who can resist the enemy and in order that the poor of the earth may be able to live under their guardianship, as there are in all realms where policy, good order, and stability exist as in Spain and other kingdoms. And if this land is to perdure, it is a great error to think that all its inhabitants shall be equal. For neither Spain nor any other kingdom would endure if it had not lords and princes and rich men. And in this land there can be neither rich nor powerful men if there be not villages in encomienda, as we have said, for all the properties and transactions are administered by the Indians of the villages which are held in the Spanish encomiendas, and apart from these there is no means whatever of additional profit.

These opinions may be easily traced to the work of Thomas Aquinas on the *Administration of Princes,* where the hierarchical view of society attains its most perfect expression. But let us not forget that the conquest of America was accomplished at a time when medieval European society was undergoing great changes, including the development of the powerful centralized monarchical states which were later to set the political tone of the modern world, as occurred in Spain from the time of the Catholic monarchs, Ferdinand and Isabella, onward. In consequence, feudal ambitions were checked by the opposing theory of royal supremacy which maintained that the new government emerging in the Americas should not be a reproduction of the old medieval type but one consistent with the modern type of centralized monarchy.

The exponents of regalism in Spain had been chiefly the jurists of the Royal Court and of the judicial tribunals charged with the defense of the King's jurisdiction against the judicial prerogatives enjoyed by the feudal lords. The Second Audiencia of Mexico, composed of five members, strongly supported this trend from the year 1530 onward. Its president, Ramírez de Fuenleal, who had a vigorous legal mind, opposed the creation of unrestricted feudal jurisdictions. He argued that the parceling out of all villages without leaving any to the Crown, reserving to it only a proportion of the income of the *encomenderos,*[1] would be a concession so excessive as to amount to treason since extensive territories and provinces, probably even larger than those inhabited by Christians, would thus be removed from the Crown's vassalage leaving it nothing but rents. In Fuenleal's opinion, it would be better for the King to grant to his subjects the tributes, rents, and personal services, whether large or small, rendered by the villages, assigning these to each grantee according to his rank; for thus, he reasoned, the Indians would understand that they were vassals of the King and that the en-

[1] The holder of an encomienda. See pp. 74–75, 80.

comenderos had nothing beyond the tribute which the Crown ordered paid to them. That is, in place of a division of the Kingdom of New Spain into feudal estates, he advocated that the King retain the sole right to jurisdiction; and if he should be pleased to grant the tributes to certain individuals, such grants would be only acts of royal grace.

The regalist point of view was again set forth in an anonymous opinion given in New Spain in 1554.

It is highly important to the interests of His Majesty [wrote the author] that a proper distribution of the Indians should be made. If they are granted to the lords, each lord will regard himself as a king. As they do not love the King and care nothing for the increase of the Crown of Spain, but think only of themselves and their families, and as they are so far away [from the seat of authority], they are within a hair's breadth of rebellion. As the experience of a few years ago showed, neither lords nor encomenderos guarantee the land [to the king]; rather, they make it ready for rebellion. If Your Majesty were to maintain a thousand men, foot and mounted, in New Spain, and an equal number in Peru, without either lords or encomenderos, all the Indians of the New World would unquestionably be quiet and obedient, and there would be no rebellions or riots. The Turks keep all their territory in safe subjection by governing them in this way, and by refusing to grant city, village, or fief to anyone. His Majesty could maintain peace and tranquillity throughout the New World and could provide for its proper spiritual instruction by giving it well-paid governors, who should be required to resume their residence in Spain after a certain brief term of office, and by sending bishops who are truly servants of God and friends of peace to care for its spiritual welfare.

The regalist ideals of the period could hardly have found a more extreme expression than this anonymous writer gave them. He wished to substitute for the particularistic system of feudal estates a centralized monarchical system administered by transient governors, who would be required to return very frequently to Spain in order that they might not forget the loyalty owed to the central government. In contradistinction to the authors who placed the strength and nerve centers of the state in feudal lordships, this political thinker preferred to rely upon a regular army of the modern type, and to this end recommended that arms be borne primarily by members of the garrisons established by the King in the principal realms of the Indies.

Moreover, the antifeudal bias of the opinion is very pronounced, for instead of representing the nobleman as a pillar of society it brands him as a source of discord and rebellion. And what is even more significant, this Christian author offers as a model to his own King nothing less than the Turkish monarchy. In the Spanish treatises of the sixteenth century there are frequent allusions to the Turkish system of government, but in most cases only to stigmatize it as a despotic regime, irreconcilable with the Christian policies that European princes should follow in accordance with the principles of divine and natural law. But, in this case, far from considering the Turk as an object of abomination, our author sets him up as a model toward which the new Spanish state in the process of creation in the Indies should strive.

Conflict between feudal and monarchical points of view was inevitable in the development of American institutions, and it developed mainly in relation to the problem of the encomiendas. One party wished to strengthen the encomienda system by perpetuating the succession thereunder and by conferring the right to administer private justice. The other party wished to deprive the institution of such attributes of feudalism.

When Cortés first instituted the *repartimientos*[1] in New Spain, he could grant them only temporarily and without the right to administer justice, for he had no authorization from the King to do otherwise. Petitions of the conquistadors for formal grants of Indian fiefs poured into the court continuously.

When the Crown sent the first Audiencia to Mexico in

[1] A distribution of Indians for purposes of labor.

1528, it offered to make repartimientos permanent and to give the Spanish holders lordship and jurisdiction over the Indians in a certain form which was to be stated at the time of making the grants. In 1530 when the second Audiencia was appointed, the Crown ostensibly intended to redeem its promise, but gave the oidores secret instructions of a regalist character, favoring the establishment of the office of *corregidor*.[1] The Crown intended to use the corregidors in opposing the pretensions of the encomenderos. Nevertheless, in 1532 the Audiencia prepared a description of New Spain containing the names of the villages, their products, the number of vassals in each, and so on, which was intended to serve as the indispensable statistical basis for making the distribution. However, the plan was not carried out at that time, and in 1536 the famous Law of Inheritance for Two Generations was passed. Under its terms, the grants from the Crown which the encomenderos were holding provisionally could pass to their legitimate descendants or to their widows for one life. This limited concession was revoked in 1542 when the New Laws were promulgated. The Crown now ordered that upon the death of an encomendero his encomienda should be declared vacant and should revert to the Crown.

The New Laws naturally produced bitter resentment among the conquistadors and their families. After several uprisings and under the continual pressure of their agents at the Royal Court, they succeeded in obtaining a revocation of the Laws in 1546.

The Crown then promised that encomiendas would be granted in perpetuity, but without judicial powers; that is, the lord or encomendero would not have the right to administer justice among his vassals. This prerogative was to be retained by the King. Viceroy Mendoza was governing in New Spain when the cedula of 1546 was received there. He believed that the Crown was disposed to fulfill its promise and therefore began the preparation of two inventories, one

[1] A Spanish official charged with the administration of a given region.

of persons and the other of villages, which were to serve as a basis for distribution.[1]

Notwithstanding the fact that the Viceroy sent these important statistical documents to Spain, the distribution of the encomiendas in perpetuity was further delayed. Extensions of the encomiendas for several lives were actually granted to the families of the encomenderos from time to time, a practice called *disimulación* (dissimulation); but the institution still remained a far cry from its archetype in Spain.

In 1550 a series of important councils was held in Valladolid to consider the question of perpetual grants. According to Bernal Díaz, who attended them, those present were told that as soon as the Emperor, who was then absent, should return, the matter would be settled in such a way that the conquistadors "would be well satisfied, and so it still remained undone." The Viceroy of Mexico, Luis de Velasco, advised the King in 1564 to make the promised settlement, for in the opinion of Velasco this would give strength and security to the land.

According to information gathered by the cabildo of Mexico in 1597, the situation regarding the encomiendas was as follows:

The status of the encomiendas of this city of Mexico and in the jurisdiction of the Audiencia which were given to the conquerors and founders of this New Spain, in remuneration and payment for their services, is that scarcely one out of four survives; and of these almost all are in the third lifetime and very few in the second. There are not thirty in this latter class and upon the death of the grandchildren of the aforesaid conquerors and founders now in possession for the third lifetime, the aforesaid encomiendas will be pronounced vacant one by one and will revert to the Crown. At the rate at which reversions to the Crown have occurred since this city of Mexico and the remaining provinces of New Spain were won seventy-five years ago, within which short

[1] Both documents have come down to us and both have been published. One of them, the *Diccionario de Pobladores,* was published by Icaza; the other, the *Suma de Visitas,* by Del Paso y Troncoso. See Bibliography.

time three-fourths of the aforesaid encomiendas have fallen vacant and expired, it is reasonable to expect that the remaining one-fourth will likewise revert within twenty or thirty years. . . .

The situation in New Galicia was very similar, to judge from the account given by Bishop Mota y Escobar.

If we shift our attention to Peru, we find that the problem of perpetual encomiendas was fully discussed in 1559. The King undertook to have assembled accurate information for solution of the problem, and sent various commissioners to study the pros and cons of the matter. The Viceroy of Peru, Conde de Nieva, and the commissioners wrote from Lima on May 4, 1562, a lengthy letter in which they analyzed the probable political results to Peru from the establishment of perpetual fiefs. The letter began with a concession to the feudal point of view in recognizing that if all encomiendas were taken over by the Crown the result would be disorder and confusion, for the flocks would be left without a shepherd. As in other commonwealths, it was essential that there should be persons of varying rank, condition, and estate, and that they should not all be equal, for as in the case of the human body "all the members are not of equal value for the right governing of the whole."

But when the authors of the opinion came to consider whether it was advisable to cede to the lords all the Indians of Peru, they recalled that the vassals of the King were better treated in Spain and elsewhere than those of the nobles. Moreover, if the principle of perpetuity were adopted, within thirty or forty years the sons, descendants, and other successors of the original feoffee would have no love for the monarchs or for Spain, or for their interests. As a consequence of birth in the Indies and of never having known the homeland and its institutions, they would be inclined rather to detest them

as generally seen and understood to be the case with those in one kingdom governed by another, even though they may be descendants of Spaniards; for the love which a man naturally bears toward the land of his birth and which springs from its soil is very great, as great or greater than that which he bears toward his parents or toward the land from which they were descended.

The foresight and good sense of this opinion of the sixteenth century are notable. In it are forecast the lines of development of American *criollo* feeling. The authors noted that in the Kingdom of Naples the children of Spanish parents "respond more willingly to the summons of the country where they were born than to the summons of Spain." In America, in the course of time, the descendants of Spaniards, they wrote, "will be as native as the Indians born there." In fact, an attempt to identify the cause of the criollo rebels of the nineteenth century, who were descendants of the Spaniards, with that of the conquered aborigines of the sixteenth century was made by a Mexican author of the period of Independence, Father Mier, although another author, Alamán, pointed out defects in the argument.

Returning to the Peruvian letter of 1562, its authors argued that the maintenance of the encomiendas in perpetuity would be irreconcilable with the dependence on the Spanish Government in which it was expedient to hold the Indies. Once such privileges were granted, the beneficiaries, naturally abhorring subjection to a kingdom that would seem to them alien, could make common cause with one another against the domination of Castile.

Such counsels as these must have made an impression on Philip II, then King of Spain, who was already following a policy of regalism in the mother country. At any rate, just as the whole sixteenth century passed without the fulfillment of the promises made to the conquistadors of New Spain in regard to the perpetuity of their encomiendas, so Philip denied the petitions of the would-be Peruvian feudatories.

Only in very special cases were *señoríos* (estates similar to those of the Spanish nobility) given in perpetuity and with judicial powers. To this class belongs the Marquesado del Valle, which was held by the family of Hernán Cortés; but the history of this grant is marked by constant limitations placed upon it by the royal authorities. In addition to the few truly noble estates, one must take into account the fact, already stated, that the Crown, by way of dissimulation, also permitted the inheritance of some encomiendas to the fourth and fifth generation; but even so, the system was very different from the medieval panorama envisioned by the conquistadors of America.

The problem of the encomienda was later complicated by the fiscal interests of the Crown, which constantly sought to acquire a larger share of the tributes paid by the Indians. By the eighteenth century these efforts had resulted in the almost total absorption of this income by the royal treasury, and the old encomiendas, or the pensions paid from the royal treasury to their former owners, continued to exist in only a few provinces.

The possibility of creating a general system of nobility in the Indies became ever more remote, and the political system of the colonies moved ever nearer to the centralized and bureaucratic type of the modern European state.

This trend became influential in the political problems of the period of independence, for both Mexican and South American leaders thought that although their people might lack a democratic tradition, they also lacked the constituent elements of a monarchy since one of the most important of these was a hierarchy of nobles.

Many years later when Maximilian of Austria was struggling to establish a monarchy in Mexico, he wrote that government by the Spanish viceroys could in no way be considered a precursor of monarchy. As the viceroys were constantly being changed, he said, they never succeeded in identifying themselves with the country, which was an indispensable prerequisite to any just comparison of their regime with the rule of the royal houses of Europe.

·VIII·

THE ENCOMIENDA AS AN ECONOMIC INSTITUTION

THE most generally accepted idea regarding the encomienda is that lands and Indians were partitioned among the Spaniards from the first days of the Conquest. Without entering into a detailed discussion of the development of the institution during the long colonial period, some authorities have held that these repartimientos became the basis of the hacienda, which, as we know, consisted of a large tract of land owned by a single proprietor and worked by a considerable number of Indian peons bound to the land. Tied by debt to their masters, it was difficult for them to change their residence or leave the estate. But this notion that the encomiendas were the true origin of the haciendas is open to serious question, both in the light of the history of the land and of the history of the people.

It is true that from the very beginnings of the colonial period there were repartimientos and grants of land as well as repartimientos of Indians to work them, but the two institutions were clearly differentiated from each other. The granting of land was customarily in the hands of the cabildos, whereas the institution of the encomienda always depended on the governor or the viceroy. When these last-named authorities also exercised the privilege of distributing lands, the titles to such lands were never confused with those of the encomiendas. Moreover, grants of land (*mercedes de tierras*), as their name indicates, related to ownership of the soil, while the grants of encomiendas (*títulos de encomiendas*) made no mention of conveying dominion of the land.

Examination of a few examples of the establishment of encomiendas will confirm these assertions. Thus, during the Spanish colonization of the Antilles, titles were granted in the following terms: "I commend to your care [the Indians] in order that you may make use of them on your haciendas and in your mines and transactions in the manner directed by their Highnesses [Ferdinand and Isabella] in their ordinances."

In New Spain, we find the following form used by Hernán Cortés in granting encomiendas:

By these presents half of the lord and natives of the village of [name] are entrusted to you [name] in order that you may make use of them and that they may aid you on your haciendas and in your transactions, according to the ordinances issued or to be issued on this subject, and you are charged to labor with them in the matter of our holy Catholic faith, with all the vigilance and solicitude necessary and possible therefor.

In the middle of the sixteenth century Viceroy Luis de Velasco of New Spain issued the following charter:

I entrust and commend to you [name] the villages of [names], together with their subjects, in order that during His Majesty's pleasure you may hold them in encomienda . . . and that you may hold and dispose of the stipulated tributes and services which the Indians of the said villages are obligated to render in conformity with the schedules already prepared or to be prepared.

In none of the above instances is property in the soil bestowed. Could this be due to carelessness on the part of the Spanish jurists? That would be hard to believe, for in true medieval fashion they used five or six words to say the same thing in their legal documents. It is more probable that if all allusion to ownership of land was absent, this was because the institution of the encomienda did not include the conveyance of such rights.

In support of our hypothesis we can cite a royal cedula of May 14, 1546, sent by Prince Philip to the Viceroy of New

Spain, Don Antonio de Mendoza. In this cedula Philip stated that he had been informed of the high rate of mortality among the Indians in the Crown villages and on the encomiendas, and that since the lords continued to demand the full tribute from the Indians, which the latter were unable to pay, the said encomenderos were entering upon the lands of dead Indians and seizing them as their own. The Prince wished to put a stop to the harm thus being done to the natives, and he ordered the Viceroy to see to it that the Spanish encomenderos should in nowise succeed to the lands and tenements left by dead Indians of the encomienda villages. In case any of the Indians should die without heirs, their property was to be turned over to the village for its enjoyment in order that the villagers might better be enabled to pay their established tributes.

Thus, the holder of an encomienda was not recognized as having any property right in the land prior to the death of the Indian occupant, nor was it admitted that the encomendero might take for his own use land that fell vacant, for the right to such land devolved first upon the heirs of the dead Indian and next, in the absence of heirs, upon the village. This corresponds to the provisions of Law 30, Title 1, Book VI, of the Recopilación, where it is stated that the encomenderos shall not succeed to the lands and tenements left vacant by the death without heirs of Indians within the encomienda, but that the villages to which they belonged shall inherit of the lands in question enough to pay and satisfy the tributes levied upon them, and somewhat more, and that whatever then remains shall revert to the Crown.

It is therefore not merely possible to distinguish between grants of land and of encomiendas, but, in addition, when we turn our attention to the problem of land titles within the repartimientos, we perceive that the Indians possessed and inherited land individually as well as collectively as members of their villages, and that if lands within an encomienda fell vacant they passed into the hands of the King and not of the encomenderos.

It is true that the encomenderos appear, in other documents, to possess ranches or other lands within the encomienda, but this was due to one of two reasons: In some cases the tribute-paying Indians, being obliged to pay the encomendero a certain quantity of corn or wheat, set apart a portion of land for the purpose of raising these products. This arrangement did not involve a transfer of the ownership of such lands. In other cases the encomendero acquired a tract of land within the bounds of the encomienda villages by means of a separate grant; but this was his by virtue of the special grant and not by virtue of his title as encomendero. Instances also occur in which the possession of and title to land within an encomienda was held by a Spaniard other than the encomendero, toward whom he was generally hostile.

In summary, we may state that in New Spain property in the soil was not conveyed by the granting of an encomienda. Within the boundaries of a single encomienda could be found lands held individually by the Indians; lands held collectively by the villages; Crown lands; lands acquired by the encomendero through a grant distinct from his title as encomendero or affected by his right to the payment of tribute in agricultural products; and lastly, lands granted to Spaniards other than the encomendero.

The foregoing demonstrates that the encomienda cannot have been the direct precursor of the modern hacienda because the former did not involve true ownership. The origin must rather be sought within the normal system of landed property, which was based on outright grants of land.

Some of the Peruvian titles of encomienda speak of deeding "all the chiefs, elders, and villages, estates and coca farms [*chácaras de coca*] which belong and appertain to them." This phrase could be interpreted as a conveyance of land, but its purpose was rather to fix the extent of the encomienda. In New Spain also the legal status of the chief town determined that of the villages and estates subject to it.

In Chile, in one instance, the encomendero of a depopulated village instead of claiming that the vacated lands belonged to him by virtue of the original title of encomienda, petitioned the royal authorities to give him title thereto by a new and distinct grant. In the case of Venezuela, a more difficult problem may be raised by certain title deeds describing the territorial extent of the encomiendas; but I do not have sufficient data to be able to determine whether or not the encomiendas in that country involved a transfer of title to the land.

The second point that we are interested in clarifying in connection with the encomienda system is whether the encomienda was a labor institution.

We have already seen how, during the colonization of the West Indies, Indians were granted to the Spaniards for service on the plantations, in the mines, and in commerce. Bartolomé de Albornoz was to write later, in his *Arte de Contratos,* that at that time the Indians were distributed by groups and not by villages. By the terms of the ordinances mentioned in the encomienda titles, the Spaniard who was granted a chief and his group of Indians could use them as laborers in mines and on farms.

Hernán Cortés and his companions had resided in the West Indies and knew the deplorable effects of the system of encomiendas based upon personal service. Therefore, when the conqueror of Mexico drew up the Indian patents in New Spain he wrote the King stating that he had not granted the encomenderos the right to take the Indians away from their villages to work wherever the Spaniards might wish. Since work in the mines had largely destroyed the natives of the West Indies, he considered himself in conscience bound not to permit the holders of encomiendas in New Spain to employ the encomienda Indians in mining. He believed that the Indians who had been enslaved would suffice for this purpose.

In spite of these restrictions, the encomiendas of New Spain played an important economic role in relation to mining. They were the food-producing centers for laborers in the mines, and they also provided the materials used in building houses and mills. This, however, was a matter of providing auxiliary services rather than of direct employment of the encomienda Indians in the labor of mining.

By 1536, in the administration of Viceroy Mendoza, silver mining had replaced gold mining to a great extent as a result of the recent discovery of huge deposits of silver. This change led to a considerable increase in the demand for labor, and the Viceroy permitted the use of encomienda Indians in mining whenever they indicated willingness to pay their tribute to the encomenderos in the form of such personal service. In these cases, tribute in goods or money was commuted to work in the mines.

This state of affairs lasted until 1549. On February 22 of that year, the Crown issued an important cedula addressed to the president and judges of the Audiencia of New Spain. In it the King stated that he had been informed that the decision to allow the Indians to pay tribute in personal service, or to substitute work in the mines or elsewhere for the payment of tributes in kind or money, had produced some very undesirable results. Many of the Indians had to travel fifty or more leagues from their own lands, loaded down with their food, clothing, and bedding; some of them fell ill and died; and teaching of the Christian doctrine was made more difficult. The cedula therefore ordered a revision of the tributes due from the Indians to the Crown as well as to the encomenderos, and also directed the cancellation of all commutations to personal service of tribute in kind or money.

The enforcement of this prohibition marked the end of the encomienda as a labor institution, for from this time forth all tributes had to be paid in money, produce, or native wares. Proof exists that the law was enforced. Just previous to the receipt of the decree, the *Audiencia de los Confines* in Guatemala had put into effect important levies which included personal service for certain villages. When the new law of 1549 reached Guatemala, the levies were changed and tribute in goods was required in place of the personal services previously stipulated. In some sections of America — in Chile and Paraguay for example – the change from payment in labor to payment in goods could not be put into practice, and tribute in labor continued for many years; but in the main, it was enforced in the viceroyalties of New Spain and Peru in spite of the resistance of interested encomenderos.

In accordance with the Recopilación of 1680, tributes of the new type could consist of money, wheat, corn, yuca, poultry, fish, clothing, cotton, cochineal, honey, fruit, vegetables, and other goods which could be conveniently collected.

The encomiendas having become an institution for collecting tribute in other forms than personal service, we must inquire on what basis the amount and nature of such tribute was determined.

Beginning with the promulgation of the Law of Inheritance in 1536, the Crown strongly supported the idea that the public authorities should regulate the tribute and not leave the matter to the will of the encomenderos. According to this law, the judges were to hear a Solemn High Mass for the purpose of enlightening their understanding before fixing the levy. Moreover, they were to consider each case without fear or favor, and after taking the required oath they were to visit personally all the Crown villages and the encomiendas. They were to ascertain the number of natives and other inhabitants of each place, the quality of the land, and also the amount that the Indians had been accustomed to pay their own chiefs and other persons who governed them prior to the arrival of the Spaniards, as well as the amount of their current contributions to the Crown or to the encomenderos. After obtaining such information they were to fix the amount of the tribute, taking care that it should be payable in goods which the Indians had or could produce on their lands. All this material was to be written down in a tribute roll, which was to be made known to the natives, to the officers of the King, and to the encomenderos.

In the Recopilación of 1680 some precepts regarding levies were included. The lists were required to be clear, distinct, and specific, detailing all that the Indians were required to pay as tribute, barring minutiae; and each village was to make its payments in two or three different kinds of goods. The weight and dimensions of the blankets they were to deliver must be specified so that they might not be required to make payment in blankets of excessive size. The Indians were to sow their crops on their own lands and not on those of the main village, and the encomendero was to bear the expense of transporting the produce. Whenever harvests were lost as a result of drought or storms, the Indians were not to be required to pay the tribute to the encomendero for that year, either then or subsequently.

The spirit of justice that inspired these laws regarding tribute is not without precedent in the history of Spain before the discovery of America. In the course of their long struggle against both secular and ecclesiastical lords, the rural classes had succeeded in having the levies required of vassals written down in the *cartas pueblas* and the *fueros*.[1] Thus it was not left to the will of the master to demand whatever goods and services he pleased, for these were stipulated in written form and made known to all.

In America, however, the natives, accustomed to their own civilization and not to that of Europe, did not have the same conception of their rights as that which prevailed among the popular classes of Europe in the beginning of the modern age. The Spanish Government tried to establish an equitable economic relationship between the encomenderos and their tributary Indians; but in practice abuses were committed by the Spaniards, and the natives had their weaknesses. Nevertheless, the idea of public surveillance over tributes and of the protection due the weak did exist, with the result that the fixing of the levies was not left to the will of the stronger party.

The requirement that the amount customarily paid by the

[1] *Cartas pueblas* were documents describing the lands and rights granted to the inhabitants of a new town. *Fueros* were the laws or municipal codes of the Middle Ages in which the privileges and exemptions of a province, city, or person were set forth.

Indians to their lords previous to the Conquest should be ascertained was likewise important. It again reveals the tendency of the Spanish Government to respect, in so far as possible, the former customs of the natives. In Mexico they had been required to pay tribute every eighty days, and in general the same period was adopted for their payments to the Spanish encomenderos. Hernán Cortés says in his will that in order to fix the amount of tribute on his estate he took great pains to find out what the ancient levies had been. The Crown also ordered very detailed information on this point to be gathered, in order to approximate as closely as possible the pre-Hispanic tribute.

In addition to fixing the levies, the authorities were accustomed to enumerate the vassals in each village in order that the amount should be in proportion to the number of Indians. These censuses are of very great value for demographic studies of the Spanish colonies.

The kind and amount of tribute which each Indian was obligated to pay varied in different regions. In some, it was easy to obtain cotton; in others, grain, and so on. But there was a trend toward the standardization of the annual payment at one peso of eight reales plus half a hundredweight of corn, the value of which in the middle of the sixteenth century was about three silver reales.

The legal ages for the payment of tribute generally extended from eighteen to fifty. The chieftains, by virtue of their rank, and the Indian *alcaldes* and *regidores,*[1] who were elected annually in each village, were exempted from payment. In some districts the women also were exempt. Border Indians just brought under Spanish control were exempted from tribute for ten years in the hope of more easily winning their allegiance. These exemptions were sometimes extended over much longer periods. The Crown used exemptions from tribute as a means of bringing about transfers of population, as occurred in 1582 when it decreed that free workers in the

[1] Local officials.

mines would not be obliged to pay tribute. This was done in order to attract laborers to the mines.

Zorita says regarding the distribution of the tribute that as a rule three-fourths of the amount went to the encomendero or to the Crown, according as the village belonged to a private encomienda or to the Crown. The remainder was used for the salaries of the caciques, the costs of administration, community expenses, and the Church. The tribute records of 1550 published by Del Paso y Troncoso contain many examples of the tributes paid in New Spain. A relatively prosperous village would pay the encomendero two thousand pesos a year, more or less, while a poor encomienda would sometimes bring in two hundred pesos a year.

As we have seen, the beneficiaries of the tribute might be either private encomenderos or the Crown. Sometimes upon the death of an encomendero the tribute might be used to pay certain pensions instead of being assigned to another encomendero. Some statistics have been preserved regarding the number of villages in the three groups of encomiendas, Crown villages, and unassigned villages. On the island of Hispaniola in 1514 there were 715 repartimientos comprising 22,344 Indians bound to service. In New Spain in 1545 there were 1,385 Spanish settlers, of whom 577 were encomenderos. In the same viceroyalty in 1550 there were 537 encomienda villages and 304 Crown villages. In New Spain in 1560 there were 480 encomienda villages paying a tribute of 400,000 pesos a year, as compared to 320 Crown villages paying a tribute of 100,000 pesos. By 1571 the number of Crown villages had increased to 359, with an estimated population of 440,000 Indians; but the income from them was not over 150,000 pesos. Thirty years later there were 140 encomienda villages in New Spain with an income of 300,000 pesos and an additional 30,000 pesos came from vacant or unbound villages.

The foregoing figures show that in the course of the sixteenth century private encomiendas decreased appreciably, while those held by the Crown increased. The income from the Crown villages was not as high proportionately as in the villages held by individuals. This was undoubtedly due to the fact that the King had to employ a large number of officials to collect the revenue from his villages.

We also have figures for other parts of Spanish America. In Peru, for example, the tributes paid by the Indians amounted in 1561 to 1,226,676 pesos. There were 427 encomienda villages and fifty that either belonged to the Crown or were unassigned. Here the system of private encomiendas was obviously stronger in comparison with that of Crown villages than in New Spain. In the Plata region and Tucumán about 1673, some 13,000 Indians were controlled by 251 encomenderos.

According to the estimates for the Indies at large, made by López de Velasco in 1574, there were then 3,700 repartimientos belonging to the Crown and to private encomenderos, with 1,500,000 tribute-paying Indians, not counting the other members of their families. Of some 32,000 Spanish families, it was estimated that 4,000 held encomiendas. In 1631 Antonio de León Pinelo estimated that the incomes from the encomiendas of all America totalled 966,228 ducats, of which 150,000 ducats came from New Spain.[1]

The Crown used various methods of surveillance over the social and economic life of the encomienda villages. Justice was administered by the representatives of the Crown (corregidor or alcalde mayor), and not by the encomenderos. The clergy who resided in the villages usually aided the Indians in defending their rights. The higher courts, including the viceroy and the Audiencias, heard the complaints of the natives and often issued writs in their behalf. It was also the practice to send visitadores to survey the districts in order to gather information regarding all kinds of injustices, especially concerning excesses in the matter of levying tribute. Some of the reports of the commissioners are still in existence, and they throw much light on life in the regions through which they passed.

[1] The colonial ducat was then worth 6 reales, or 337 maravedis; while the Spanish ducat was worth 375 maravedis. Both were worth less than the *peso de minas* of 8 reales, which was worth 450 maravedis.

The law did not permit the encomendero to dispose of his tribute rights to another person. Laws 16 and 17, Title 8, Book VI, of the Recopilación prohibited all transactions of this kind. The right of succession to an encomienda also possessed a unique character, for it was governed by the terms of the grant and not by the general rules of inheritance. Antonio de León wrote as follows on this point:

The encomiendas are not hereditary properties, but statutory grants (*legales*), or, under the feudal law, entails. Thus, succession to the title is not by right of inheritance, but according to the provisions and stipulations of grants authorized by statute (*ley*). Were this not the case, the wife of the first holder could not succeed, should there be living sons or grandsons of the first holder, or uncles and nephews of the second holder; nor could any collateral descendants, who are in fact totally excluded, be debarred from intestate succession. The succession, then, is determined by the statute which directs that on the death of the first encomendero the encomienda shall pass *ipso jure* either to the one next in degree or to him who may be appointed to succeed, without the requirement of previous acceptance, petition, or other positive act; and provided that the succession thus acquired is not to a bare right to possession but to a title (*posesión misma*), as under an entail, equivalent to the fullest succession under Roman praetorian law.

In order to complete the economic picture of the encomienda, it is also important to bear in mind the taxes imposed by the Crown. These included half-annates, payments for the support of the fleet, assessments to pay the salaries of the Council of the Indies, a payment to the royal treasury, and so on. These expenses greatly diminished the money value of the encomienda.

From the time of the accession of the Bourbons to the Spanish throne early in the eighteenth century, the Crown's interest in gaining possession of the income from the encomiendas greatly increased. By a cedula of November 23, 1718, it was ordered that all the unassigned or unconfirmed encomiendas, as well as those which in the future should fall vacant, should revert to the Crown, and that the tributes should be paid into the treasury offices of their respective districts. After the established pensions and other charges on these encomiendas had been met, the remainder was to be used to defray the expenses of the treasury offices in question.

Naturally there were some protests against this measure. Certain provinces, such as Yucatan, succeeded in obtaining postponements or exemptions; but the Crown finally absorbed virtually all of the income from tributes. Thus the Spanish government itself put an end to this institution which played so important a rôle during the century of the Conquest. When the Cortes of Cadiz, which met in 1811–12 on the eve of the Spanish-American wars of independence, discussed at length the problem of feudal estates in Peninsular Spain, it was not obliged to adopt any special policy regarding this problem in America, for with a few exceptions, such as the marquisate in Mexico belonging to the family of Hernán Cortés, the problem no longer existed there.

· IX ·

THE EVOLUTION OF THE LABOR SYSTEM

UNTIL the middle of the sixteenth century the labor system in New Spain rested upon slaves, who were employed mainly in the mines and at other hard tasks, and upon the personal service rendered on the encomiendas by way of tribute. Both forms represented a system of unpaid labor. Naturally, no wages need be paid to slaves. As for the services rendered to the encomenderos in that early period, these were based upon the theory that the Indians in their encomiendas owed them tribute as vassals, and the personal service that they performed was regarded as a part of their tribute. Consequently, these were likewise a type of unremunerated labor.

The problem of native labor was completely changed when about the middle of the sixteenth century the slaves were freed and, in accordance with the cedula of February 22, 1549, personal service under the encomienda system was prohibited and the encomenderos were henceforth permitted to collect tribute only in kind or in money. It fell to Viceroy Luis de Velasco to struggle with the serious problem raised by this great change in the institutions that had provided the labor supply of New Spain since the beginning of the Conquest. Through what channel would the labor necessary for carrying on the work of the colony now be obtained? Would it be possible to establish a system of voluntary wage labor like that in use in Spain?

Hardly thirty years had passed since the conquest of Mexico brought two completely different civilizations into contact with each other — the European civilization of the sixteenth century and the Indian civilization of the period of Moctezuma. It was therefore easy to foresee that the European system of voluntary wage labor would not function satisfactorily as a means of regulating all labor relations between the two groups. Nevertheless, in the instructions of April 16, 1550, the Crown charged Viceroy Velasco to attempt to persuade the Indians to hire out for labor in the cities and the country so that they might not be idle. The enforcement of this order was to be in the hands of the royal authorities in the colony; private Spaniards would have no power to compel the Indians to work even if the Indians belonged to their encomiendas. The Viceroy was to require that their wages be paid to the Indian laborers themselves and not to their chiefs or to any other person. The labor was to be moderate, and those who exacted excessive labor were to be severely punished.

The aim, therefore, was to establish a system of voluntary wage labor with moderate tasks; but in anticipation that the Indians might not offer their services voluntarily, the order further directed the royal authorities in the colony to deliver laborers to colonists who needed them. From one point of view this order was designed to prevent abuses arising from a direct relationship between the Spanish master and the Indian laborer, as shown by the clause forbidding the encomenderos to compel the Indians to work. From another point of view, however, its significance lies in the fact that if the effort to establish a voluntary system of labor should fail through the Indian's refusal to accept work, the state was ready to act as a mediator and to protect the public interest by compelling the laborer to work.

As the economic needs of the European group, accustomed to the agricultural, commercial, and industrial life of sixteenth-century Europe, were greater than those of the Indians, it was certain that there would always be a great demand for labor. On the other hand, as the Indians did not have the same interest in this more highly developed economic life and as their inherited techniques were not the same as those of the laboring classes of Europe, there was inevitably a perpetual maladjustment between the labor supply and the needs of colonial society.

To all this can be added the incompatibilities of language and religion and the other social and cultural differences between the two great nuclear groups which made up Mexican society. All this explains why the Crown's hopes of shifting immediately from slavery and tribute in personal service to voluntary wage labor were not realized. Outlines of a compromise system — one in which labor was enforced by the governors but was remunerated by wages — began to take shape even during the administration of Viceroy Velasco. Under this system the justices or *jueces repartidores* summoned the Indian workers and assigned them to labor on farms, in mines, on public works, and in the domestic service of colonial society.

This was the origin of what was called in New Spain the *cuatequil* or system of forced wage labor. This system, combined with previous indigenous customs, was to develop on a much larger scale in Peru under the name of *mita,* an institution distinct from both slavery and the personal service of the encomienda, both of which were displaced in the process that we are describing. The advantage to the Indian of this new form of labor as compared with the previous system was that he received a daily wage and that public authorities moderated the hours and the character of his labor. On the other hand, coercion could not be abandoned although voluntary labor was gradually beginning to make its appearance in certain types of work.

The principle advanced by Spanish jurists to justify coercive intervention of the authorities in labor relations rested upon a concept of public interest. They maintained that without Indian labor colonial life could not develop, and that the state could not compromise with general idleness. But the interpretation of public interest given by these writers and by the laws was not confined to public works, but also included, as contributory to the general welfare, the farms, mines, buildings, and other private enterprises of the colonists.

The main differences between the cuatequil of New Spain and the mita of Peru lay in the fact that the former usually affected Indians in districts near the place of work, while in Peru the laborers had to travel much greater distances. In New Spain the work period was almost always one week and each Indian presented himself for work three or four weeks a year. The Peruvian periods of labor lasted for months. The quota of workers raised by the villages of New Spain was commonly 4 per cent, and in Peru one-seventh, or about 14 per cent. In Tucumán one Indian was taken out of every twelve.

The list of people eligible to obtain labor in this way usually included the clergy, the Spanish authorities, and the Indian chieftains, in addition to the Spanish colonists. In the distribution of workers even the lands of the University of Mexico were given preference to other farms

> in order that natives who dedicate themselves to study may be encouraged and strengthened to carry on their work and also in order to aid the sons and conquistadors of this New Spain who wish to apply themselves to the study of their choice, whereby it is well known they can gain much honor and profit.

With regard to mining in New Spain, there was a restriction which forbade the use of these Indian laborers, or *tapisques* as they were called, in the interior of the mines. They were employed mainly in the smelting of metals in the mills. The other work was done by the *laboríos,* or voluntary Indian laborers, who usually earned good wages and were given a share of the metal they obtained, and who came to specialize in mining labor.

The extension and consolidation of the system of compulsory wage labor characterized the period covering the administrations of Velasco (1550–1564), Martín Enríquez (1575–1580), and other viceroys up to the beginning of the seventeenth century. In the end it became the chief source of labor in the colony. Not even the encomenderos succeeded in remaining independent of the institution of the cuatequil. If they needed laborers, they could no longer take them directly from their villages as they had formerly done as a form of tribute. Like other private colonists, they were forced to apply to a justice or a juez repartidor for the number of Indians needed, and the workers thus provided no longer worked gratuitously but were entitled to customary wages from the encomendero.

The Indians of the encomienda villages were, moreover, subject to the obligations of this general system of compulsory labor, so that if the authorities in charge thought it advisable to turn them over to someone other than the encomendero, the latter had no right to contest or impede such assignment.

In the preceding chapter we noted that the encomienda carried with it no title to the soil, and we now see that the encomendero lost control over the labor of his Indians since this was regulated independently by the royal authorities.

In the period between 1575 and 1600 an important increase in the wages of the Indians took place. In the beginning they had been paid half a real a day; later, common laborers were paid a real and artisans two reales. The latter were the masons, carpenters, smiths, or other men who knew a trade. The pay was subsequently increased to a real a day and board for the unskilled worker, or one and a half reales. Thus, the amount of the daily wage was tripled.

The liberal ideas which were already active on behalf of the Indians in the middle of the sixteenth century, when they were freed from slavery and from personal service to the encomendero, resulted in a new agitation against the system of compulsory labor. Writers of this persuasion asked themselves if this system was compatible with the free status of the Indians, notwithstanding the reasons of state and public interest advanced in its justification which had already given rise to laws on vagrancy in the European countries.

This movement succeeded in modifying the legislation on

the subject, for in 1601 and 1609 new cedulas were issued for the purpose of establishing voluntary, and of putting an end to compulsory, labor for wages. The jueces repartidores were replaced by *comisarios de alquileres,* who were to watch over labor relations but who could not deliver Indians to employers without first consulting the wishes of the laborers. The Indian could now go to the public squares to hire out to whomever he wished, and the only requirement was that he might not remain idle. The Crown expressly stated that its wish was that the natives might live in complete liberty as its vassals, in the same way as its other vassals in the Indies and in Spain.

The colonial authorities, fearing the effects that this change might produce in American economic life, did not enforce the laws with any rigor; in fact, compulsory labor continued. In 1632, however, the Crown repeated the prohibition during the administration of Viceroy Cerrato in New Spain and finally brought about the suspension of all assignments of compulsory labor except in the case of mines.

The effects of the new measure upon agricultural labor were not serious because for years past the Spanish farmers had begun to attract to their farms the Indians of the neighboring villages who were known as *gañanes* or *laboríos.*[1] Thus, instead of waiting for the periodic assignment of Indians by the public authorities, they had Indian families continuously in residence on their own lands as laborers. This provoked conflicts between the Spanish farmers and the Indian villages, for the latter resented the diminution of the number of their people available for compulsory service before this was abolished and the corresponding increase in the amount of work that devolved upon Indians who remained

1 In Spain at the time of the colonization of America, *gañán* signified a person who did agricultural or pastoral work for wages. In New Spain the term was commonly applied to Indians who left their town to settle on the estates of Spaniards, where they worked at farming and stock-raising. Their families usually settled permanently on these estates, and their descendants continued to render the same kind of service. In colonial documents *laborío* and *naborío* had the same meaning as *gañán.*

in the village. Consequently the authorities ordered that the gañanes established on the farms of the Spanish colonists should not be exempted from personal service (cuatequil) when their turn came; but it was also permitted that at such times their own employers could retain their services, which would then be debited against the total amount of forced labor to which the employers were entitled as farmers. Hence, when compulsory farm labor was abolished by Cerrato in 1633, the owners of farms already had other sources of labor supply. Moreover, the landowners had begun to do everything in their power to strengthen their hold on their gañanes by depriving them of freedom to leave the farm at will. The legal means of accomplishing this purpose was found in advances of money and goods, which bound the gañán to the land by placing him in debt. This method, and not the old encomienda of the sixteenth century, constitutes the true precursor of the Mexican hacienda of more recent times. Under the latter system the master is the owner of the land through grant, purchase, or other legal title, or perhaps only as a squatter, and he attracts the gañanes to his lands and then keeps them there by means of debts.

Liberal thought in the period of colonization did not fail to look with mistrust upon this system of agrarian servitude through debt, and it denounced the system as formerly it had denounced slavery, the encomienda, and the cuatequil. The Spanish government made significant provisions for limiting the amount of legal indebtedness. For example, at one time it permitted the advance of not more than three months' wages to the rural workers. Again, it limited the sum that could be advanced; this was not to exceed five pesos, and the landowner would lose whatever he advanced above this amount, for no right to collect it was recognized.

Some measures were taken to assure that the wishes of the Indian should be respected if, in spite of his debt, he should desire to move to another estate. Generally the new master paid the debt to the former landowner, and by this means an Indian with well-founded complaints could change residence.

On the other hand, the first master was protected when his worker left him without cause and without paying his debts to make an agreement with another landowner.

In spite of all these legal restrictions, an examination of the legal character of the Mexican rural system in the eighteenth century reveals that the farmers had succeeded in extending the system of gañanía and had secured it by means of debt. There were even some cases involving estates with a large population in which, after the royal treasury collected from the owners or their stewards the tribute due from the gañanes to the King, the owner added this debt to those arising from his own advances of money and of goods and used the aggregate debt to bind the worker to his estate.

The growing number of peons and the isolation of estates gave rise gradually to the custom of punishment of the peons by the master or his representatives; but this does not mean that the latter possessed judicial authority, for the King's justice intervened whenever a serious crime was committed.

The system of peonage thus had colonial roots, but in that period the vigilance of the public authorities afforded a measure of protection to the laborers. When, subsequently, laissez faire or other abstentionist theories of public law left the peons alone and defenseless against the economic power of their masters, the harshness of the hacienda regimen increased, and the population and importance of the Indian villages steadily diminished in comparison with the estates employing peons.

We have already said that compulsory labor in mines persisted beyond the year 1633, but that the number of free workers attracted by the relatively high wages of miners increased. The public authorities artificially stimulated this trend when they exempted mine workers (laboríos) from the payment of tribute. It should be noted that it was greatly to the interest of the mine operators to have a regular corps of skilled and diligent Indians for mining work, since the gangs of forced labor assigned to them by the authorities were composed of Indians who knew little about mining and the continual weekly shifting of these gangs interfered with the normal course of operations. Moreover, as we have already remarked, these tapisques could not be legally employed in the underground labor of the mines. Consequently, the mine operators themselves were determined that there should be free, wage-earning labor residing on the properties.

The device of juggled indebtedness functioned in the mines as well as on the haciendas, and foremen sometimes traveled great distances to recover fugitive laborers. Legally, advances of pay could not amount to more than eight months' wages. Many conflicts were caused by the practice followed by some employers of enticing Indians away from others by offering them more money or better working conditions. Legislative policy was always opposed to this practice because it left the first operator without labor and with unpaid Indian debts.

The consummation of the process of replacing the forced laborer (tapisque) by the free laborer for wages (laborío) was witnessed by Alexander von Humboldt when he visited New Spain at the beginning of the nineteenth century. It was for this reason that he wrote that the work in the Mexican mines was performed by free labor.

Sugar mills presented serious labor problems. The government very soon imposed limitations upon the use of forced Indian labor in these mills; and, in line with its restrictive policy, it even went so far as to forbid the construction of new mills. Land could not be devoted to the planting of sugar cane without a previous certification that such land was unsuitable for the planting of corn or wheat, and only in such case was the planting of sugar cane permitted.

The official explanation of the restriction of Indian labor in the mills was the harm suffered by natives performing that type of work. The evidence shows that economic as well as humanitarian considerations were involved. The Crown recommended that millowners buy Negroes to take the place of the Indians and even forbade the Indians to hire out voluntarily for such labor.

The industry of cloth mills also was important. These consumed the wool produced on the large sheep ranches manufacturing certain fabrics that were sold in domestic trade. In spite of copious legislation favoring free labor in these infant industries, the work in them was in fact a rigorous form of servitude. The laborers lived a life of close confinement, like those who worked in bakeries and tanneries. Generally they were bound by a system of indebtedness, although some of them were convicts. The criminal branch of the Audiencia of Mexico was empowered to sell convicted felons into service in the cloth mills, and the sentences could run for several years. Humboldt professed to be particularly distressed by the working conditions that he observed in this industry.

Among the workers in the cloth mills were many Chinese who came from the Philippines by way of Acapulco. The slave traffic in Orientals came to have a certain importance in New Spain, although in the seventeenth century they were ordered to be set free. Perhaps the presence of these laborers explains some of the influences noted in the style of Mexican fabrics.

The improvement of labor conditions in the cloth mills was not the only concern of the Crown in this matter. In accordance with the mercantilist policy, which tended to favor manufacturing in the mother country at the expense of that in the colonies, it imposed a series of restrictions on the types of fabrics whose manufacture was permitted in colonial mills and on their sale. Likewise, a close watch was kept over the erection of new establishments.

In summary, in the face of many obstacles the system of colonial labor progressed from slavery, from unpaid personal services in lieu of tribute, from forced labor, and from debt peonage, toward a standard of free paid labor, that is, toward the economy common to the modern world.

As a rule, the colonial stage of Hispanic-American history has been thought of as one characterized by great tranquillity and by a minimum of problems. This idea, however, is perhaps due to the preference that has been given to political history as understood by the nineteenth century, and to the neglect of social history. For as soon as we fix attention on the tremendous problems of organization and labor presented by the period of colonization, this illusion is at once dispelled; and in its place we see a spectacle of constant change in the basic structure of the labor system – a social phenomenon manifestly of exceeding interest.

· X ·

SPANISH COLONIZATION AND SOCIAL EXPERIMENTS

IF the traditional, static picture of Spanish colonization had not so long enjoyed credit, the subject we are about to discuss would call for no introductory remarks. The social experiments of which we shall speak did not all belong to a single type, nor were they related to one another; but they did have some features in common. In the first place, all were deflections from the usual type of Spanish-American society created by the Conquest and by the subsequent complicated interplay of feudal aspirations and the racial heterogeneity existing between conquerors and conquered. In the second place, all represented a bold search for forms of social life better suited to the declared purposes of protecting the natives or of improving mankind in general.

Each of these experiments had a well-defined character of its own. They occurred throughout the whole course of Spanish colonization in America and in many different regions. Consequently the deviations from type which we are about to discuss deserve to be considered by historians along with the common and much more familiar type of social adjustment between Europeans and Indians.

The first case to consider involved Aristotelian rationalism and the experimental measurement of the rational capacities of the Indians. In our discussion of the nature of the American man which took place from the beginnings of colonization, we have already seen that Aristotelian theory of rational differences between men was opposed to the Christian doctrine, sustained principally by Las Casas, of the essential equality of all men. We have also noted that while these theoretical disputes were going on, contradictory reports reached Spain concerning the actual cultural status of each group of Indians as it was discovered.

This aggregate of theory and factual information not only had academic value but also influenced the choice between freedom and tutelage as the basic principle of the institutions under which the aborigines were to live during the Spanish regime.

The first statement of the problem of the encomiendas revealed these preconceptions. When Cardinal Cisneros, Regent of Spain, decided to send three Jeronymite friars to the island of Hispaniola as governors in 1516, his instructions to them pointed out three possible solutions for the problem of governing the Indians. The friars were, first, to determine whether it would be possible to organize free Indian villages which would be tributaries of the King. If they found that this system of Indian autonomy was not feasible, the formation of villages administered by Spaniards was then to be tried. If this solution should also prove unfeasible, the encomiendas were to be maintained.

When the Jeronymite friars arrived in Hispaniola, they circulated an interrogatory or questionnaire designed to give the Spanish inhabitants an opportunity to express their ideas regarding the capacity of the Indians. One of the questions was as follows:

> Does the witness know, believe, or has he observed or heard it said that these Indians, especially those of Hispaniola, women as well as men, are of such knowledge and capacity that they should be given complete liberty and that they would be able to live politically? Would they know how to support themselves by their own efforts, each Indian mining gold, tilling the soil, or maintaining himself by other daily labor? Do they know how to care for what they may acquire by this daily labor, spending only for necessities, as would a Castilian laborer?[1]

[1] With very slight changes, the translation of this passage follows the one in Lewis Hanke, *The First Social Experiments in America,* p. 29.

The witnesses were also to give their own opinion as to whether it was advisable to let the Indians live as freemen in the existing villages, or in others that might be established, under a salaried Spanish governor; or whether it would be better to leave them in the encomiendas, and in the latter case whether any reforms were necessary in the encomienda system.

In this way, Cardinal Cisneros hoped to obtain valuable advice regarding this problem from persons who had a personal acquaintance with native society in the West Indies. Many of the witnesses, however, had a special interest in the final decision regarding the system of government for the Indians, and their views were by no means favorable to the suppression of the encomiendas, which might result if they admitted that the aborigines possessed complete political capacities. Aside from the influence of these special interests, the European way of life was so different from that of the West Indian natives that it was easy for the colonists to believe that the capacity of the Indians really was inferior to that of the average Spaniard.

The upshot was that the Jeronymite friars maintained the system of the encomiendas, to the great indignation of Las Casas.

This solution of the problem was not definitive, and when Charles V assumed active control of the Spanish Government he had a number of Indians set apart in villages in order to afford an opportunity for determining by actual experience and observation whether they could live as freemen. The decision would now depend not upon more or less suspect testimony but upon social experimentation. Two such villages were established during the administration of the Licentiate Figueroa in Hispaniola, and in a letter of July 6, 1520, he reported to the King as follows:

> The two villages of Indians that I have established as a means of testing their capacity for political life do lazily what is necessary in order to eat, and no more. Up to the present they have done nothing more than begin to learn how to extract gold for the

payment of the levy of three pesos per head to your Majesty. I have given them the tools and other necessary things. . . . They are making some progress, although they do almost no work. I do not believe they will have the ability to do it properly in the time given them, for they take no heed of advice, although they are told that they will be free if they do so; . . . There is nothing to be lost if they go on in this way for a while, for no injury will be done to a third party since all of them belonged to your Majesty and the Admiral [Diego Columbus]. Even if they do nothing but remain as they are, to live and multiply, something will be gained. As for the Indians in the encomiendas, everyone admits that they will very soon be done for, no matter what is done to protect them; but that to take them away from the Christians would surely bring about the depopulation of the island.

Figueroa was hardly optimistic. Nevertheless, in 1520 the Emperor decided to extend the system of liberty to all the natives of the islands, and the results of this policy have been examined in detail in some modern studies. The importance of the measure decreased because the Indian population of the West Indies was soon reduced to a very small number; but some of the observations and principles established at this time were subsequently a factor in the organization of Spain's continental possessions in America.

Moreover, from the point of view of social history it is a noteworthy fact that a colonizing state of the sixteenth century, when in doubt regarding the capacities of the natives and the institutional system suitable for governing them, did not cling exclusively to abstract principles or procedural formalities, but gave the aborigine an opportunity to demonstrate his capacities experimentally.

The second phase of this question to which I wish to call attention is that of the missions and their communal organization. In various parts of the far-flung Spanish empire, a traveler passed quickly from kingdoms organized according to the ordinary civil standards of Hispano-Indian society to other regions where only members of religious orders were found administering the Indian mission villages, and where

Spanish civil society had not penetrated or was far from having the preponderance it enjoyed in other zones. Besides their intrinsically religious character, these missionary regions presented forms of social organization that cannot be neglected by anyone who wishes to obtain a complete picture of Spanish experience on our continent.

We have seen that while the conquest and exploration of America were in progress, stubborn doctrinal disputes took place over the question whether it was permissible first to establish dominion through the agency of secular colonists and then proceed to the propagation of the faith, or whether Spain should give the whole undertaking a pacific missionary character, entrusting it to the religious orders either alone or with only a small military force for their protection.

Las Casas was the most resolute champion of the latter method, and he not only defended it in his treatises but put it into practice in the region of Verapaz, situated in Guatemala, which was inhabited by heathen Indians who had resisted the intrusion of the Spaniards. The Dominican friars, headed by Las Casas, succeeded in persuading the Crown to prohibit secular Spaniards from entering this territory, which accordingly became first an experimental center for attracting the Indians to the faith by purely peaceful means and thereafter a mission zone.

Almost all the religious orders that administered the American missions adopted important features of communal organization. The latter was not unknown in Hispano-Indian civil society, as is proved by the existence of communal funds and by the fact that some crops, industrial products, and other forms of wealth were owned in common by the Indian villages — a system that provided large means for the common welfare. However, communal life was more vigorous in the missions. The rudiments of private Indian property could occasionally be found in the missions, but they were not the basis of the most characteristic and important form of organization, which revolved about the priest. Besides his spiritual functions, the priest acted as an administrator in the temporal field. He kept the tools and implements for farming and building. He kept the seed, supervised the work, and kept an inventory of the livestock. All the Indians cultivated the mission lands, and the products were gathered together in a common granary from which the priest drew out what was to be sold or used for new plantings and as food for the Indians who labored for the community.

The tutelage exercised by the priest over the Indians naturally embraced their religious life as well. He was also their physician, teacher, adviser, judge, and not infrequently the stern arbiter when questions of labor and punishments were involved. A prosperous and well-managed mission was known by the abundance of its crops and livestock and the good appearance of its buildings and ornaments.

This system was applied to tribes that had scarcely any notion of sedentary life, such being usually found on the borders of the civilized Spanish zones.

There was no lack of criticism of this type of social organization. Sometimes the criticism came from secular clergy who wished to supplant the religious orders; sometimes from laymen impatient to penetrate the mission zones and assimilate them to the central Hispano-Indian districts. When criticism was disinterested, it was directed against the excessively paternalistic power exercised by the priests and the scant opportunity for individual initiative that was left to the Indians.

It is true that in comparison with the viceregal centers, where individualistic legal principles operated, life within the missions was under a relatively paternalistic and communal system. The missionaries, however, always defended the efficacy of this type of administration as a means of colonizing the less civilized Indian regions and of impressing upon the neophytes the rudiments of civilized life.

The reasons for the adoption of this type of organization are still a matter of doubt. Some authors speak of the influence of communal life as practised by the monastic orders in Europe. Others believe that the method was adopted in view of the undeveloped human material available for improvement in these colonizing zones. There are some historians who trace the origin of the system to Indian customs. Another possible explanation lies in the influence exerted upon the most distinguished members of the religious orders by their reading or by other cultural currents.

Another form of colonization that deserves attention is the one which sought to develop in America the ordinary type of Spanish farmer. Favorable references to this type of settlement occur frequently in Spanish royal documents of the period.

In 1513 King Ferdinand ordered Pedrarias Dávila to take farmers to Darién to experiment with the cultivation of Spanish condiments, wheat, barley, and other grains. Certain privileges were to be granted to anyone undertaking this work. In 1523 Charles V wrote to Hernán Cortés that the officials of the *Casa de la Contratación* of Seville would take great pains to promote the emigration of farmers and laborers to New Spain and would also send Cortés plants, trees, and seed. In 1531 the emigration of farmers from Spain to the West Indies was encouraged, for the decline of the population of the islands was by now alarming. In 1533, sixty farmers and their families arrived in the city of Santo Domingo. Philip II even permitted Portuguese farmers to emigrate to Spanish America, and in his *Ordenanzas de Población* of 1573 he repeated his desire that laborers should emigrate to the Indies.

Some members of religious orders, like Las Casas, wished to utilize colonization by farmers to offset that of a military character which had spread over America. Las Casas expounded this plan with perfect clarity when he spoke of the desirability of sending real settlers, that is, those who should live by tilling the rich lands of the Indies, lands which the Indian owners would voluntarily grant to them. The Spaniards would intermarry with the natives and make of both peoples one of the best commonwealths in the world, and perhaps one of the most Christian and peaceful. This would be far better than sending over indiscriminately all kinds of profligate people to plunder and destroy the New World.

The Crown accepted this plan, and Las Casas personally took charge of recruiting the emigrants. Traveling from Zaragoza to Castile, he described to the people of the towns through which he passed the richness of the American soil. Some were ready to join him because they hoped to get rich; others because they were peasants on feudal estates and wanted to leave their children free land, dependent only on the Crown, like the land in America that they had heard about from Las Casas. Naturally, the Spanish lords were opposed to the abandonment of their lands by these farmers, but the King gave Las Casas not only legal support but financial aid. In the end, however, the experiment collapsed when Las Casas' squire absconded with the funds.

Two years later, in 1520, he repeated the attempt and collected funds contributed by fifty inhabitants of the West Indies who were to be the impresarios of the organization. After obtaining the King's consent, Las Casas recruited farmers in Spain, choosing such plain and humble people as would be congenial to the simplicity and gentleness of the Indians. By dint of great effort the expedition succeeded in making a settlement on the coast of Paria, but the Indians rebelled and again the experiment ended in failure.

Las Casas regarded this as a divine punishment for having associated himself with men who helped and favored him not for the sake of God or through zeal for saving the souls that were perishing in those regions but only because of their greed for riches, whereby he had offended God by this blot upon the purity of a wholly spiritual enterprise.

Perhaps the true causes of the difficulty of establishing farmers in the Indies consisted in wresting them from the feudal estates of Spain; in the cost of transporting them and supporting them until the first harvest; and in the difficulty of their living with the local Indians, who were sometimes warlike, and who, in case they were peaceful, tempted the European immigrant to refuse to do personal work and instead to turn himself into a master of the native laborers. The Government, moreover, could not bring itself to spend any great amount of money to encourage this type of emigration when there were so many people who went to the Indies willingly, and at their own expense, in the military expeditions.

Peaceful colonization by farmers and artisans did not become the normal and general pattern of the emigration of Spaniards to America during the first decades of the colonial period. Nevertheless, the existence of this pattern cannot be ignored, whether as a corrective of the other type of emigration or, when the stage of conquest had ended, as a continuous flow of humble settlers removing from the motherland to the colonies to engage in various kinds of labor. This is very clearly illustrated in some regions, such as northern Mexico, where the aristocratic and bureaucratic type so familiar in the population centers of both Mexico and Peru did not easily prosper. Together with some representation of the latter type, for it was not completely absent, we find primarily a plain European people who did their own work.

The fourth and last type of social experiment to which reference should be made is that of Renaissance utopianism in relation to America. Of all the social ideas and experiments developed in the course of Spanish colonization, this type stands out as one of the noblest.

The Renaissance had provoked in Europe a deep yearning for a different and better social world. Disgusted by the greed and warfare of their own age, the humanists delighted in the thought of the Golden Age of which the ancients spoke, and described in utopias the ideal world toward which mankind should direct its footsteps. This movement, represented principally by Sir Thomas More and later by Campanella, also drew vigor from the immortal fount of Platonism.

Property, labor, religion, wars, and luxury, and indeed every conspicuous item of the social problems of the period, were subjected to scrutiny. Individualism and the commercial spirit were beginning to dominate European modes of life, but utopianism aspired to communal norms of property which would substitute love of humanity, virtue, and moderation for egoism and conflict.

It was while these ideological problems were germinating that America became known to Europe. The tales of the navigators, especially of Vespucius, made a deep impression. In the New World were living naked, simple, ingenuous peoples who typified the Golden Age toward which the humanists aspired. The more perfect spiritual world painted in the utopias could now be brought to earth in a favorable environment. The bold and enterprising mind of Vasco de Quiroga made the essential advance to the position that the simple world of American aborigines was predestined to government under the standards of Renaissance utopianism. Thus, More's *Utopia* was to be transformed into a Magna Carta of Hispano-Indian society. The task of the European should not be to transport to America *his* values, in order there to reproduce the same tortured society from which the humanist was fleeing, but to avail himself of the unformed and tractable mass of Indian population in order to produce from it the perfect Christian commonwealth.

A more elevated ideal of colonization is inconceivable. Enfolding the American Indians in its optimism, Spanish humanism proposed to eliminate exploitation and selfish paternalism from their life and raise it to the most exacting social standards of that time. Viewed in this light, America was not a new world in the sense of geographical discovery but in the sense of its promise for mankind.

Spanish humanists even believed that the Government would make this program its own. It did not do so, but the idea did exist as one part of the aggregate of Spanish thought about America. It may also be set down as one of the Spanish social experiments in America because Vasco de Quiroga, in addition to expressing his aspirations in writing, founded two institutions in the neighborhood of Mexico City and Michoacán which he called hospitaler-villages of Sante Fé, to which he gave as ordinances the principles contained in More's *Utopia*. These included the community of goods, the integration of families in groups of various married couples, the alternation of urban and rural life, work for women, a six-hour working day, a liberal distribution of the products of common effort according to the needs of the inhabitants, the abandonment of luxury and of useless offices, and a local, elective magistracy.

In conclusion, I shall be satisfied if I have succeeded in making clear in this book the reasons that exist for believing that the Spanish colonization of America was characterized by a rich social ideology and a substantial amount of experimentation. The subject is one that can be studied with profit if we renounce the prejudices that have long made it seem an inert mass of historical facts and a period of slight constructive significance.

SELECT BIBLIOGRAPHY

Only works which have been consulted in the preparation of this volume are cited in this bibliography.

Anuario de la Asociación Francisco de Vitoria. Madrid, 1929–34. (Contains various indispensable monographs on the ideas of the Conquest.)

Aquinas, Thomas. *Regimiento de los Príncipes.* Valencia, n. d. (Biblioteca de Tomistas Españoles. vol. V).

Barrasa y Muñoz, José. *La colonización española en América.* Madrid, 1925.

Bate, John P. *Francisco Vitoria and His Law of Nations.* Oxford, 1934.

Bolton, H. E. "The Mission as a Frontier Institution in the Spanish-American Colonies." *American Historical Review,* XXIII (1917), 42–61.

Bullón, Eloy. *El doctor Palacios Rubios y sus obras.* Madrid, 1927.

Castillo de Bobadilla, Jerónimo. *Política para corregidores y señores de vasallos en tiempo de paz y de guerra.* Madrid, 1775.

Chacón y Calvo, José M. "La experiencia del indio," in *Anuario de la Asociación Francisco de Vitoria,* V, 203 ff.

Davenport, F. G. *European Treaties Bearing on the History of the United States and Its Dependencies.* Vol. I, Carnegie Institution of Washington, 1917. (Of interest for the study of the bulls of Pope Alexander VI.)

Díaz del Castillo, Bernal. *Historia verdadera de la conquista de la Nueva España.* Mexico, D. F., 1939.

Eppstein, John. *The Catholic Tradition of the Law of Nations.* London, 1935.

Fonseca, Fabián, and Carlos de Urrutia. *Historia general de Real Hacienda.* Mexico, 1845–1853.

García Icazbalceta, Joaquín. *Don fray Juan de Zumárraga.* Mexico, 1881.

Hanke, Lewis. *The First Social Experiments in America.* Cambridge, Mass., 1935.

—— "The 'Requerimiento' and Its Interpreters." *Revista de Historia de América.* Mexico, D. F., 1938. No. 1, pp. 25–34.

Humboldt, Alexander von. *Ensayo político sobre el Reino de la Nueva España.* Mexico, D. F., 1940.

Icaza, Francisco de. *Diccionario autobiográfico de conquistadores y pobladores de Nueva España.* Madrid, 1923.

Las Casas, Bartolomé de. *Apologética Historia de las Indias.* Madrid, 1909.

—— *Colección de Tratados.* Buenos Aires, 1924.

—— *Del único modo de atraer a todos los pueblos a la verdadera religión.* Mexico, D. F., 1942.

Lauber, A. W. *Indian Slavery in Colonial Times within the Present Limits of the United States.* New York, 1913.

León Pinelo, Antonio de. *Tratado de Confirmaciones Reales.* Madrid, 1630.

Leturia, Pedro. "Las grandes bulas misionales de Alejandro VI." *Bibliotheca Hispana Missionum,* I. Barcelona, 1930.

Levene, Ricardo. *Introducción a la Historia del Derecho Indiano.* Buenos Aires, 1924.

Levillier, Roberto. *Gobernantes del Perú. Cartas y papeles. Siglo XVI.* Madrid, 1921 and later. 14 vols.

López de Velasco, Juan. *Geografía y descripción universal de las Indias.* Madrid, 1894.

Marchant, Alexander. *From Barter to Slavery. The Economic Relations of Portuguese and Indians in the Settlement of Brazil, 1500–1580.* Baltimore, 1942.

Mota y Escobar, Alonso de la. *Descripción geográfica de los reinos de Nueva Galicia, Nueva Vizcaya y Nuevo Leon.* Mexico, D. F., 1940.

Nys, Ernest. *Droit international et politique.* Paris-Brussels, 1896. (Of interest for the study of the bulls of Alexander VI.)

Ots y Capdequí, José M. *Instituciones sociales de la América española en el período colonial.* La Plata, 1934.

—— *El estado español en las Indias.* Mexico, D. F., 1941.

Parry, J. H. *The Spanish Theory of Empire in the Sixteenth Century.* Cambridge, England, 1940.

Paso y Troncoso, Francisco del. (ed.) *Papeles de Nueva España.* Madrid, 1905–1906.

—— (ed.) *Epistolario de Nueva España*. Mexico, D. F., 1939–40.

Ríos, Fernando de los. *Religión y estado en la España del siglo XVI*. New York, 1927.

Saco, José A. *Historia de la esclavitud de los indios del Nuevo Mundo*. Havana, 1932.

Sahagún, Bernardino de. *Historia general de las cosas de Nueva España*. Mexico, D. F., 1941.

Sepúlveda, Ginés de. *Tratado sobre las justas causas de la guerra contra los indios*. Mexico, D. F., 1941.

Simpson, L. B. *The Encomienda in New Spain*. Berkeley, 1929.

—— *Studies in the Administration of the Indians in New Spain*. Berkeley, 1938.

Solórzano Pereira, Juan de. *Política Indiana*. Madrid, 1930.

Staedler, E. "Die Donatio Alexandrina und die Divisio Mundi von 1493." *Archiv für katolisches Kirchenrecht*. Mainz, 1937. 3 und 4, pp. 363–402.

Vander Linden, H. "Alexander VI and the Demarcation of the Maritime and Colonial Domains of Spain and Portugal, 1493–1494." *American Historical Review*, XXII (1916), 1–20.

Vanderpol, Alfred. *La doctrine scolastique du droit de guerre*. Paris, 1925.

Viñas Mey, Carmelo. *El estatuto del obrero indígena en la colonización española*. Madrid, 1929.

Vitoria, Francisco de. *Relecciones teológicas*. Madrid, 1917.

Wölfel, J. D. "Alonso de Lugo y Compañía. Sociedad comercial para la conquista de la isla de La Palma." *Investigación y Progreso*. Madrid, VIII, nos. 7–8, July and August, 1934, pp. 244–48.

Zavala, Silvio. (See below, Author's Bibliography.)

Zorita, Alonso de. *Breve y sumaria relación de los señores y maneras y diferencias que había de ellos en la Nueva España*, etc. *Documentos Inéditos del Archivo de Indias*, II, 103 ff.

AUTHOR'S BIBLIOGRAPHY

I. BOOKS: *Los intereses particulares en la Conquista de la Nueva España,* Madrid, 1933. *Las instituciones jurídicas en la Conquista de América,* Madrid, 1935. *La Encomienda Indiana,* Madrid, 1935. *La "Utopía" de Tomás Moro en la Nueva España y otros estudios,* Mexico, D. F., 1937. *Francisco del Paso y Troncoso. Su misión en Europa.* 1892–1916. Mexico, D. F., 1938. *Fuentes para la Historia del Trabajo en Nueva España.* Compiled in collaboration with María Castelo. Mexico, D. F., 1939–41 (5 volumes, and others in preparation). *De encomiendas y propiedad territorial en algunas regiones de la América española,* Mexico, D. F., 1940. *Ideario de Vasco de Quiroga,* Mexico, D. F., 1941. *Independencia* and *México contemporáneo,* in volumes 7 and 11 of the *Historia de América,* directed by Ricardo Levene, Buenos Aires, 1940–41.

II. ARTICLES: "El tercero en el Registro mejicano," in *Revista Crítica de Derecho Inmobiliario,* Madrid, Sept. 1932, Year VIII, No. 93, pp. 701–10; Oct. 1932, Year VIII, No. 94, pp. 737–47; Nov., 1932, Year VIII, No. 95, pp. 829–40. "Las conquistas de Canarias y América," in *Tierra Firme,* Madrid, 1935, Year I, No. 4, pp. 81–112, and 1936, Year II, No. 1, pp. 89–115. "La propiedad territorial en las Encomiendas de Indios," in *Universidad,* Mexico, Sept. 1937, vol. IV, No. 20, pp. 34–37. "Genaro Estrada y la Historia de México," in *Letras de México,* No. 18, Nov. 1, 1937, pp. 1–2, 10, 12. "Indigenistas del Siglo XVI," in *Sur,* Buenos Aires, No. 42, Year VIII, March, 1938, pp. 73–76. "La nueva biografía de don Lucas Alamán," in *Letras de México,* No. 24, Feb. 1, 1938, p. 4. "Las encomiendas de Nueva España y el gobierno de don Antonio de Mendoza," in *Revista de Historia de América,* Mexico, No. 1, March, 1938, pp. 59–75. "Los trabajadores antillanos en el siglo XVI," in *Revista de Historia de América,* No. 2, June, 1938, pp. 31–67; No. 3, Sept., 1938, pp. 60–88; No. 4, Dec., 1938, pp. 211–16. "Letras de Utopía. Carta a don Alfonso Reyes," in *Cuadernos Americanos,* Mexico, No. 2, March–April 1942, pp. 146–52, 10 facsimiles.